Quick & Easy

Turkish

Necdet Teymur
B.Arch, M.Arch, PhD

G000065519

TEACH YOURSELF BOOKS
Hodder and Stoughton

Contents

Introduction

How to Speak Turkish

Introduction to Turkish Grammar

Contents

Introduction

This course of self study aims to help you to understand and speak simple Turkish, the sort of Turkish you will need on a visit to Turkey. It can't promise that at the end you will be speaking perfectly but, by enabling you to learn the most important words and expressions a visitor needs, it will undoubtedly help to improve your experience of Turkey and get more out of your time abroad.

It does not require a great deal of study or concentration, but it does offer more than a phrase-book and you will find that if you are prepared to spend a certain amount of time, even at odd hours of the day, in going through each unit in turn and testing your knowledge carefully, you will begin to acquire a basic knowledge of the language. You will find 20 units, each dealing with a particular aspect of a visit to Turkey. Within each unit are groups of words and phrases with English translations. Look at them carefully and read them aloud, referring where necessary to the Pronunciation section. Make sure the stress is correct. Then turn the page and do the written exercises on a separate piece of paper. You will find the answers in the Answer section after the units.

The questions are of two types: those which require a test of memory, to see whether you have remembered how to ask a question or say a phrase which has been printed on the page before, and those which ask you to adapt a given phrase or sentence to suit your *own* purposes. For example, in Unit 13 on the subject of food you will find the expression **Ben şeftaliyi severim** (*I like peaches*). Turn the page and you will see that you are asked to say you like several different things (all of them listed on the previous two pages). If you can do this, you have passed the 'acid test' of learning a language, which is being able to adapt given language patterns to whatever situation *you* choose.

At the end of each unit is a short information section in English.

Readers who are interested in how the Turkish language works will find the Introduction to Turkish Grammar of use. In it is a brief description of some of the most basic aspects of grammar, but only those elements which are illustrated in the course. A careful study of the Pronunciation section is essential, because, although there can be no substitute for listening to Turks talk their own language, it is possible to give a fairly good written approximation of individual sounds. It is a good idea to read both these sections before starting the course and then to refer back to them frequently.

How to Speak Turkish

The main characteristics of the Turkish language (**Türkçe**):

1 It is an agglutinating language; a Turkish word is made up of an unchanging root and one or more suffixes variously representing the idea of the subject, the plurality, the tense, etc. (e.g. *Al*abilirmiyim? *Can I take?*; *Çağı*rırmısınız? *Can you call?*).

2 It has some additional letters, mainly with special markings, and an 'i' without the dot: ç, ğ, ı, ö, ş, ü, and less frequently, â, î, û.

3 It is governed by vowel harmony which gives Turkish its grammatical and musical quality. The type of vowel in the first syllable of a word generally determines the vowels in the subsequent syllables (e.g. *bur*ada, *men*dilim, *gör*medim). This applies to suffixes too (e.g. odama, gemide, içkili).

4 Accent and stress are variable, but generally, the stress falls on the first syllable, and the last syllable has a rise in pitch especially in questions (e.g. n*asılsınız*?).

5 In spoken Turkish, words are linked together and pronounced almost as one when the first word ends in a consonant and the second begins with a vowel. This makes the words sound extremely long, but a request to say it again slowly, **Lütfen yavaş söylermisiniz?**, often solves the difficulty!

Bir otel arıyorum: *sounds like* Bi *ro* te *la* rı yo rum (I'm looking for a hotel).
Telefon edebilirmiyim: *sounds like* Te le fo *ne* de bi lir mi yim (Can I phone?).
Başım ağrıyor: *sounds like* Ba şı *mağ* rı yor (I have a headache).

Turkish pronunciation

Letter	Pronunciation	Example
A a	as in father	arka, araba
B b	bell	ben
C c	joy	cankurtaran
Ç ç	chalk	çarşı
D d	date	deniz
E e	met, bay	ekmek
F f	fell	fatura
G g	get	gel
- ğ	(not separately pronounced, but lengthens the preceding vowel)	dağ, yağ, diğer
H h	ham	hela, hamam
I ı	circus	ılık
İ i	ring, meet	istasyon
J j	measure	jeton
K k	king	kapalı
L l	lemon	limon
M m	man	masa
N n	next	nerede
O o	open	orada
Ö ö	Goethe	ön
P p	park	para
R r	rain	raf
S s	see	sarı
Ş ş	shell	şarap
T t	tell	telefon
U u	bull	uzun
Ü ü	museum, few	üzüm, Türkiye
V v	vest	var
Y y	yes	yemek
Z z	zoo	zaman

[There is no Q, X or W in the Turkish alphabet, but they are recognised by Turkish people and are occasionally used in borrowed foreign words.]

Introduction to Turkish Grammar

1 The definite article (*the*) and gender
There is no definite article in Turkish, and no distinction of gender. **O** stands for *he*, *she* and *it*. In both cases, the context suggests the 'definiteness' or the person referred to.

2 The indefinite article (*a/an*)
Bir stands both for *a/an* and for *one*: **bir oda** (a room), **bir kişi** (one person).

3 The plural
The suffixes **-ler** and **-lar** are added to the root before any other suffixes: **İngilizler** (the English), **masalar** (tables), **dağlardan** (from the mountains).

4 I, you, he, she, . . .
ben	I	**biz**	we
sen	you (informal)	**siz(-ler)**	you (plural/formal)
o	he, she, it	**onlar**	they

Ben İngilizim (I am English)
Onlar Müzeye gidiyorlar (They are going to the Museum)

5 My, your, his, . . .
benim	my	**bizim**	our
senin	your (informal)	**sizin**	your (plural/ formal singular)
onun	his, her, its	**onların**	their

Ben onun kocasıyım (I am her husband)
Sizin adınız ne? (What is your name?)

6 This, that
bu this **Bu benim arabam** (This is my car)
şu, o that **O plaj güzel** (That beach is good)
Şu bey Türk (That gentleman is Turkish)

7 To, for
Suffixes **-a/-e** (with a **y** inserted as a 'buffer' between a word ending in a vowel and the suffix)

bana to me, for me	**otele** to the hotel
bakkala to the grocer	**arabaya** to the car

8 From, out of
Suffixes **-dan/-den** (or **-ten/-tan**)

Londra'dan from London	**denizden** from/out of the sea
nereden? from where?	**cüzdanımdan** from my wallet

9 In, on, at
Suffixes **-de/-da** (or **-te/-ta**)

kitapta in the book	**otobüste** on/in the bus
Gümrük'te at the Customs	**dükkanda** in the shop

10 Of
Suffix **-in** (or **-nin**)

otelin hotel's . . .	**Jane'nin** Jane's . . .
uçağın . . . of the airplane	**paranın** . . . of the money

11 Sound changes and linkages in adding suffixes
The above suffixes change slightly depending on the ending of
the words to which they are joined, e.g.:

araba:	arabaya	arabada	arabadan	arabanın
şehir:	şehre	şehirde	şehirden	şehrin
yemek:	yemeğe	yemekte	yemekten	yemeğin

12 Adjectives
An adjective precedes the noun, as in English, e.g. **sıcak yemek**
(hot meal), **güzel manzara** (beautiful scenery), **erken uçak** (the
early flight). Indefinite articles (i.e. **bir** *a/an*) come between the
adjective and the noun, e.g. **ağır bir valiz** (a heavy suitcase),
tehlikeli bir yol (a dangerous road).

13 Verbs
(a) Infinitive; **-mek/-mak** (to . . .)

gelmek	to come	**içmek**	to drink
doldurmak	to fill	**konuşmak**	to speak

When suffixes are added for different tenses, etc. only the stem of
the verb is used, dropping **-mek** or **-mak**.

(b) To be

Ben -(y)im	I am	**Biz -(y)iz**	we are
Siz -siniz	you are	**Siz -siniz**	you are

O -dir   he/she/it is   **Onlar -dir(ler)**   they are

Ben iyiy*im* (I am well). *Onlar* uzakta*dır*lar (They are far away).
Biz Ankaralı*yız* (We are from Ankara).

(c) To be (negative): **değil** + personal suffix
Ben iyi değil*im* (I am not well). *Onlar* uzakta değil*ler* (They are
not far away). *Biz* Ankara'lı değil*iz* (We are not from Ankara).

(d) To be (question): **mi** + personal suffix
Ben iyi*mi*yim? (Am I well?). Onlar uzakta(lar)* *mı*? (Are they
far away?). Biz Ankara'lı*mı*yız? (Are we from Ankara?).
(*optional).

(e) Tenses: it is not possible here to cover all the tenses in detail.
The following are some examples of common phrases or
sentences in different tenses that you will come across in this
book:

Present:	**Türkçe konuşurum**	I speak Turkish
Present Continuous:	**Otele gidiyoruz**	We're going to the hotel
Past:	**Çok fotoğraf çektim**	I took a lot of photographs
Future:	**Yarın İzmir'e uçacağız**	We'll fly to İzmir tomorrow

14 Negative/No

The negative of verbs is made by adding **-me/-ma** to the stem,
e.g. **almak** (to buy), al*ma*dım (I didn't buy); **anlamak** (to
understand), anla*ma*dım (I didn't understand); **içmek** (to
drink), iç*me*yiz (we don't drink). The negative of *to be* verbs, i.e.
not to be, is made by inserting **değil** before the appropriate form
of **-im**, e.g. **aç olmak** (to be hungry), ben aç *değil*im (I'm not
hungry).

    Hayır means *no* and, as in English, it can either be used on its
own in informal conversation or, more generally, at the
beginning of a sentence, e.g. **Hayır, istemiyorum** (No, I don't
want it); **Hayır, teşekkür ederim** (No, thank you); **Hayır, ben
Susan Miller değilim** (No, I'm not Susan Miller).

15 Questions

Questions usually start or end with the following:

ne?	what?	**nerede?**	where?
neden?/niçin?	why?	**nereden?**	from where?
kim?/kimin?	who?/whose?	**nereye?**	to where?
kime?	to whom?	**kimden?**	from whom?
ne kadar?	how much?	**ne zaman?**	what time?
nasıl?	how?	**nereli?**	where from?
kaç tane?	how many?		(*town,*
hangi?	which?		country)

Nereden aldınız? Where did you buy it from?
Kim o? Who is he (she, it)?
Otobüs nereden kalkıyor? Where does the bus start from?
Bu kilim ne kadar? How much is this kilim?
Siz nerelisiniz? Where are you from?

16 Can/cannot

For *can*, use the stem + **(y)ebil-/(y)abil-**. For *cannot*, **-ebil-** is not used. Instead, **-e/-a** is inserted before the negative **-me/-ma**; e.g. **gelmek** (to come), Bugün gel**e**mezler (They cannot come today). Other examples:

okumak	**okuyabilmek**	**okuyabilirim**	**okuyamam**
(to read)	(to be able to read)	(I can read)	(I cannot read)
yüzmek	**yüzebilmek**	**yüzebilir**	**yüzemez**
(to swim)	(to be able to swim)	(she can swim)	(she cannot swim)

17 To have

Var means *have*, *there is*, exists, e.g. **Param var** (I have money); **Burada bir hırsız var** (There is a thief here).

Yok means *have not*, *there isn't*, *doesn't exist*; e.g. **Bilgim yok** (I have no information/knowledge); **O lokantada yer yok** (There is no room/table in that restaurant).

18 With/without

For *with*, **-ile/-le** is added to the noun or the subject, e.g. O benim**le** yüzüyor (She is swimming with me); fıstık**lı** baklava (baklava with pistachio/pistachio baklava).

-siz means *without*, e.g. Araba**sız** gidemeyiz (We can't go without the car); Bugün hava rüzgar**sız** (It is not windy [without wind] today).

19 And/or

And is **ve**:

İzmir ve Bursa'ya gidiyoruz (We're going to İzmir and Bursa).

Or is **veya** or **ya da**:

Araba yeşil veya mavi idi (The car was green or blue).

Salı ya da Çarşamba günü dönüyoruz (We're returning/going back on Tuesday or Wednesday).

NB: This section is meant to be a very brief introduction to the Turkish language and its grammar to enable the reader to use more efficiently the various sections of the book. Those who wish to improve their Turkish to a more advanced level would be advised to study books such as *Teach Yourself Turkish* by G. L. Lewis (Hodder & Stoughton) or *Colloquial Turkish* by Y. Mardin (Routledge).

1 General Expressions

a. Yes, No **b.** Hello, Goodbye **c.** Please, Thank you **d.** Mr, Mrs **e.** This, That **f.** I, My . . .

| **a.** evet | *yes* |
| hayır | *no* |

| Evet efendim./Peki efendim. | *Yes sir (or madam).* |
| Hayır efendim. | *No sir (or madam).* |

b. günaydın	*good morning* (early morning only)
iyi günler	*good day/hello*
iyi günler	*have a nice day* (while departing)
iyi akşamlar	*good evening*
iyi geceler	*good night*
merhaba	*Hello*
hoşçakalın/Allahaısmarladık	*Goodbye*

Günaydın.	*Good morning.*
Nasılsınız?	*How are you?*
Teşekkür ederim, siz nasılsınız?	*Fine thanks, and you?*
Hoşçakalın.	*Goodbye.*
Hoşgeldiniz.	*Welcome.*
Yolculuğunuz nasıl geçti?	*How was your journey?*

c. teşekkür ederim/mersi — *thank you*
  sağolun — *thank you* (informal)
  lütfen — *please*
  pardon/özür dilerim — *excuse me/sorry* (to apologise)
  affedersiniz — *excuse me* (to draw attention)
  buyrun — *welcome/come in/help yourself/ please start/can I help you?/ here it is*

Pasaportunuz lütfen.	*Your passport please.*
(Çok) teşekkür ederim.	*Thank you (very much).*
Birşey değil./Rica ederim.	*Not at all./You're welcome.*
Müsaadenizle./Müsaade edermisiniz?	*With your permission./May I have your permission?*

d. adam/erkek — *man*
  bay (Bay)/bey — *gentleman (Mr)*
  kadın — *woman*
  bayan/hanım (Bayan) — *lady, young lady (Mrs, Miss)*
  erkek çocuk, kız çocuk — *boy, girl*
  çocuk(lar) — *child(ren)*
  bebek — *baby*

Sayın . . .	*Dear . . .* (name, formal)
Bay . . ./(or first name) . . . bey*	*Mr . . .*
Bayan . . ./(or first name) . . . hanım*	*Mrs . . ./Miss . . .*

e. bir — *a/an/one*
  bu/bunu (bunlar/bunları) — *this/this one (these/these ones)*
  o/onu (onlar/onları) — *That/that one (those/those ones)*
  . . . var — *there is . . ./there are . . .*

bir valiz	*a suitcase*
bu valiz, o valiz	*this suitcase, that suitcase*
Bu valizde ne var?	*What is in this suitcase?*

*Surnames on their own are seldom used in Turkish in addressing people (except in airports or banks, etc.). Formal address is with first name + **bey** or **hanım**, e.g. **Ahmet bey, Güler hanım**.

1 General Expressions

f. **ben** — *I*
siz (formal)/**sen** (informal) — *you*
benim/benimki — *my/mine*
sizin/sizinki — *your/yours*

İsminiz ne?	*What is your name?*
Ben	*I'm ... ...*
eşim ... *or* kocam ...	*my husband ...*
eşim ... , *or* karım ...	*my wife ...*
arkadaşım ...	*my friend ...*
Bu sizin valiziniz mi?	*Is this your suitcase?*
Evet, benim valizim.	*Yes, it is my suitcase.*
Hayır, benim valizim değil.	*No, it isn't my suitcase.*

1 You are Mr Miller. A lady asks: **Siz Bay Miller'misiniz?** What do you answer?

2 You are Mr Miller. A man asks: **Siz Bay Jackson'musunuz?** What do you answer?

3 You are Mrs Miller. A man asks: **Siz Bayan Miller' misiniz?** What do you answer?

4 You are Mrs Miller. A lady asks: **Siz Bayan Jackson' musunuz?** What do you answer?

5 How do you greet a man during the day?

6 How do you greet a lady during the day?

7 How do you say 'Goodbye' to a man?

8 The customs official would like to see your passport. What does he say?

9 How do you say 'Thank you' to a man?

10 How do you say 'Excuse me' to a lady?

11 Mrs Miller would like to introduce her husband George. What does she say?

12 Mr Miller would like to introduce his wife Val. What does he say?

13 Someone offers you a drink. What do you say if (a) you want to accept?; (b) you want to refuse?

— Courtesy in Turkey requires the use of **bey** (for a man) and **hanım** (for a woman) after the first name. Surnames are not used to address people, except in airport announcements or at banks, etc., or together with the first name when addressing someone you have not met before. If the name is not known, you can call a man simply **beyefendi**, and a woman **hanımefendi** (usually shortened to **hamfendi**).

> Merhaba Emel **hanım**.
> Siz Orhan **bey**misiniz? (*Are you Mr Orhan?*) (*first name*)
> Iyi günler, siz Ayla Kutlu'musunuz? (*Good day, are you Ayla Kutlu?*)
> Siz Tracy Martin'misiniz? (*Are you Tracy Martin?*)
> İyi günler **beyefendi**.
> Affedersiniz **hamfendi**.
> Teşekkür ederim **efendim**. (*to man or woman*)

— Turkish people shake hands each time they meet and also when saying goodbye. When you are introduced to someone, you should say:

> Memnun oldum efendim (*pleased to meet you . . .*), nasılsınız? (*how are you?*)

— Here are some useful expressions and commonly used words:

Bu çok . . . *It* (or *this*) *is very . . .*

Bu oldukça . . . *It is fairly . . .*

Bu daha . . . *It is more . . .*

Bu az . . . *It is less . . .*

iyi *good*	**pahalı** *expensive*
kötü *bad*	**ucuz** *inexpensive, cheap*
büyük *big, large*	**erken** *early*
küçük *small*	**geç** *late*
kolay *easy*	**açık** *open*
zor *difficult*	**kapalı** *closed*
ağır *heavy*	**yakın** *near*
hafif *light*	**uzak** *far*

Ben *I*	**Biz** *we*
Sen *you*	**Siz** *you* (plural and formal singular)
O *he, she, it*	**Onlar** *they*

. . .**-le** *with . . .* (**Bu bey benim***le*. *This gentleman is with me.*)
. . .**-li** *with . . .* (**O izin***li*. *He's got permission.*)
. . .**-siz** *without . . .* (**Giriş para***sız*. *Free entry.*)

2 Arriving in Turkey

a. Customs b. Documents c. Nationality

a. gümrük/gümrük memuru	*customs/customs officer*
deklare (etmek)	*(to) declare*
bagaj	*luggage*
araba	*car*
arabanın bagajı	*the boot of the car*
çanta	*handbag/shoulder bag*
valiz/bavul	*suitcase*

Gümrüğe tâbi birşeyiniz var mı?	*Do you have anything to declare?*
Hayır efendim, yok.	*No sir, I do not.*
Bu sizin bagajınızmı?	*Is this your luggage?*
Lütfen valizinizi açarmısınız.	*Open your suitcase, please.*
Çantanızı açarmısınız lütfen.	*Open your (hand)bag, please.*
Tabii.	*Of course./That's OK.*
Tamam, buyrun./ Gidebilirsiniz.	*That's it, you may go./Go on.*

b. pasaport	*passport*
arabanın evrakları	*car registration papers*
ehliyet	*driving licence*
ad(ınız)/isminiz	*(your) name*
soyadı(nız)/soy ismi(niz)	*(your) surname*
kimlik/hüviyet	*identity (card)*

Pasaportunuz lütfen.	*Your passport, please.*
Adınız?	*What is your name?*
Adım . . .	*My name is . . .*
Nerede yaşıyorsunuz?	*Your place of residence?*

c.

tabiiyet/uyruk/milliyet	*nationality*
T.C. (Türkiye Cumhuriyeti)	*Republic of Turkey*
Türkiye	*Turkey*
Türk/Türkiyeli	*Turk/Turkish*
Türkçe (dili)	*Turkish (language)*
Anadolu (Kuzey, Güney . . .)	*(Northern, Southern . . .) Anatolia*
Büyük Britanya	*Great Britain*
İngiltere	*England*
İngiliz/İngiltere'li	*English (person or things), British*
İngilizce	*English (language)*
Amerika, A.B.D.	*America, U.S.A.*
Amerikalı	*American*
İrlanda/İrlandalı	*Ireland/Irish*
İskoç(ya)	*Scot(land)*
Galler Bölgesi/Galli	*Wales/Welsh*
Avustralya(lı)	*Australia(n)*
Kanada/Kanadalı	*Canada/Canadian*
Fransa/Fransız	*France/French*
Fransızca	*French (language)*
Alman(ya)	*German(y)*
İtalya/İtalyan	*Italy/Italian*
Yunanistan/Yunanlı, Rum	*Greece/Greek*
Sovyetler Birliği	*Soviet Union*
Suriye(li)	*Syria(n)*
Kıbrıs/Kıbrıslı	*Cyprus/Cypriot*
elçilik	*embassy*
konsolosluk	*consulate*

İngiliz misiniz?	*Are you English?*
Evet, İngilizim.	*Yes, I am English.*
Anlamadım.	*I don't understand.*
İngilizce biliyormusunuz?	*Do you speak English?*
Türkçe bilmiyorum.	*I don't speak Turkish.*
Çok az Türkçe biliyorum.	*I speak very little Turkish.*
İngiliz gazeteleri var mı?	*Are there any English newspapers?*

2 Arriving in Turkey

What are these called in Turkish?

3   What does the customs official ask you?

4   You have nothing to declare. What do you answer?

5   The customs official would like you to open your boot. What does he say?

6   The customs official would like you to open your suitcase. What does he say?

7   The border guard asks you your name. What do you say?

8   The border guard would like to see your passport. What does he say to you?

9   The border guard would like to see your driving licence. What does he say?

10 You don't understand. How do you reply?

11 The border guard asks: **Siz İngilizmisiniz?** How do you answer?

12 The border guard is satisfied. What does he say?

What are these three countries called in Turkish?

13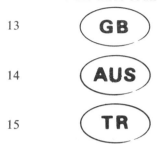

14

15

16 You would like to buy an English newspaper. How do you ask the shopkeeper if he has any English newspapers?

- British, US, Canadian, Australian, Cypriot and EEC natinals do not need a visa to visit Turkey for a holiday up to 3 months long. Others should check with their local Turkish Consulate.

- You are advised to check on customs allowances and purchase of duty-free goods before setting out on your trip.

- Embassies:
  The addresses of some embassies in Ankara:
    British, Şehit Ersan Cad. 46/A, Çankaya. Tel. 127 43 10.
    US, Atatürk Bul. 110. Tel. 126 54 70.
    Australian, Nenehatun Cad. 83, Gaziosmanpaşa. Tel. 139 27 50.
    Canadian, Nenehatun Cad. 75, Gaziosmanpaşa. Tel. 127 58 03.

- If you are driving in Turkey, you need to carry with you the vehicle's log/registration book, a valid driving licence (international advisable especially if driving a hired car) and current international insurance certificate – green card (**yeşil kart**) (fully comprehensive cover is advisable). This is sufficient for visits up to three months. For longer periods you must have a 'triptyque' that is obtainable from the Turkish Touring and Automobile Club, or from your insurance company. You are not normally allowed to sell or otherwise leave your car in Turkey. (*For further information on driving in Turkey, see the next section*).

3 Driving a Car

a. Vehicles **b.** Roads **c.** Service Stations
d. Parking

a.	**araba/otomobil**	*car*
	karavan	*caravan*
	kamyon	*lorry*
	Ağır Vasıta/Ağır Araç	*Heavy Vehicle*
	Uzun Araç	*Long Vehicle*
	trafik	*traffic*
	trafik ışıkları	*traffic lights*
	Trafik Polisi	*Traffic Police*
	araba sür(mek)	*(to) drive a car*

kiralık araba	*car rental*
Hadi İzmir'e gidelim.	*Let's go to İzmir.*
Yollar nasıl?	*How are the road conditions?*

b.	**yol**	*road*
	otoyol	*motorway*
	Ücretli Yol	*toll road*
	Mecburi İstikamet	*Diversion*
	Yol Tamiratı	*Roadworks*
	Dikkat	*Caution*
	Tehlike	*Danger*
	yol hakkı	*right of way*

yol ver	*give way*
Yavaş	*Slow Down*

ana yol	*major road/main road*
tali yol	*side road*
Ankara yolu	*The road to Ankara*
İyi yolculuklar	*Have a good journey!*

c. benzin (servis) istasyonu — *service station*
benzin — *petrol*
dizel — *diesel*
yağ — *oil*
lastik(ler) — *tyre(s)*
Sigara İçilmez! — *No Smoking!*

Süper?/Normal?	*4 Star?/2 Star?*
Ne kadar?	*How much?*
20 litre lütfen.	*20 litres, please.*
Doldurun lütfen.	*Fill it up, please.*
Yağa bakarmısınız lütfen.	*Check the oil, please.*
Ne tuttu?	*How much does it come to?*

d. park yeri/garaj — *parking/car park*
bekçili garaj — *guarded car park*
park et(mek) — *(to) park*
Park Yapılmaz — *No Parking*
araba tamircisi — *garage*
arıza(lı)/bozuk — *fault(y)/ broken down*

What are these called in Turkish?

1   2

3   Driving a Car

3   The petrol station attendant wants to know whether you would like 4-star or 2-star petrol. What does he ask you?

4   How do you ask the attendant to fill it up?

5   How do you ask him to check the oil and the tyres?

6   The service station attendant wishes you a good journey. What does he say?

Explain in Turkish what the following traffic signs mean:

7   8   9   10

11   Where does the scene in this picture take place?

— **Traffic rules and road signs** conform to the International Protocol, and are fairly similar to those in the UK. In Turkey cars drive on the right, and the 'give way' rules are a combination of the priority of those on the main road and those coming from the right. Road markings are not always clear or comprehensive. When overtaking, never cross the unbroken lines. As a general rule, be extremely careful on all the roads. (*See also information box in Unit 20.*)

There are good quality roads between major cities, and moderate ones between small towns. Motorways, or express roads (**otoyol**), are fairly recent and do not yet cover the whole country.

— **Speed limits:** 50 km/h (31 mph) in a town, and 90 km/h (62 mph) outside urban areas. Avoid night driving if possible.

— **Seat belts** are compulsory in the front seats.

— **Petrol:** there are two grades, **süper** (4-star) and **normal** (2-star), both of which are available everywhere. Service stations (**benzin istasyonu**) can be found even on remote roads, and some have restaurants attached to them which are open round the clock.

— **Parking** is restricted in cities, but easier in smaller towns. There are privately run parking lots in city centres. Traffic is regulated by the traffic police (**Trafik Polisi**). Fines are imposed on the spot for any traffic offence.

— **Rescue service (Kaza servisi):** there is no comprehensive rescue service comparable to the AA or RAC, and those that do operate are concentrated on the E-5, the Edirne-İstanbul-Ankara route. (*See also the information box in Unit 20.*)

4 Finding Your Way

a. Maps **b.** In town **c.** Streets **d.** Directions

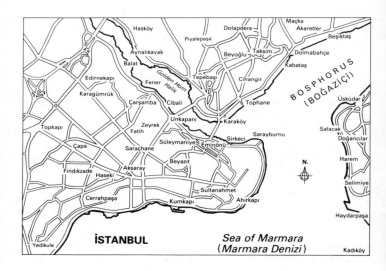

a. **harita** — *map*
   şehir haritası — *city (street) map*

| Karayolları haritanız var mı acaba? | *Do you have a road map, please?* |
| Bir İstanbul haritası lütfen. | *A map of İstanbul, please.* |

b. **şehir/kent** — *town/city*
   Vilayet — *town hall (Mayor's Office, provincial government)*
   Belediye — *town hall (Municipality)*
   kasaba — *small town*
   köy — *village*
   ev — *house*

Ankara kenti	*The city of Ankara*
şehir merkezi/centrum	*city centre*
şehir turu	*sightseeing tour*

c.

cadde	*street (main)*
sokak	*road*
bulvar	*boulevard/avenue*
tek yön	*one-way street*
meydan	*square*
köprü	*bridge*
trafik ışıkları	*traffic lights*
trafik işaretleri	*road signs*
Geç	*Go (pedestrians)*
Dur	*Stop (wait)*

Atatürk Bulvarı nerede acaba?	*Where is Atatürk Avenue?*
Nerede kalıyorsunuz?	*Where are you staying?*
Laleli'de Kumru Oteli'nde.	*At the Kumru Hotel in Laleli.*
Eviniz nerede?/Nerede yaşıyorsunuz?	*Where is your house?/Where are you living?*
Barış Sokak, 3 numarada.	*At 3 Barış Road.*

d.

yön/istikamet	*direction*
. . . nerede?	*Where is . . .?*
viraj	*bend*
dönüş/dönülmez	*turn/no turning*
sola dönüş (yok)	*(no) left turn*
sağa dönüş (yok)	*(no) right turn*
doğru gidiniz	*straight ahead*
kuzey	*north*
güney	*south*
doğu	*east*
batı	*west*

Bursa yolu hangisi acaba?	*Which way to Bursa, please?*
Affedersiniz, Cumhuriyet Caddesi nerede acaba?	*Excuse me, where is Cumhuriyet Street?*
Doğru gidin.	*Go straight on.*
Sola dönün.	*Turn left.*
Sağa dönün.	*Turn right.*
Çok uzak mı?	*Is it (too) far?*
Hayır, oldukça yakın.	*No, it is quite near.*

Weights and Measures→7, Places of Interest→15, Excursions→16

4 Finding Your Way

1 What does each letter stand for in Turkish?

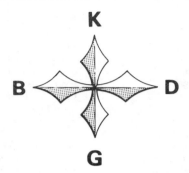

2 You want to buy a street map of İstanbul. What do you say?

3 You want to buy a road map. How do you ask for it?

4 You want to know how to get to Karaköy. What do you say?

5 How do you tell someone to turn right?

6 How do you tell someone to turn left?

7 How do you tell someone to go straight ahead?

8 You want to know if it's far. What do you say?

9 Which word do you see on the pedestrian signal when it is red?

10 Say the names of the major Turkish cities and tourist resorts: İstanbul, Ankara, İzmir, Bursa, Konya, Antalya, Alanya, Antakya, Marmaris, Bodrum, Van, Edirne, Trabzon.

11 You want to cross the Bosphorus Bridge. Which lane do you get into?

— Maps (**harita**), town plans, lists of hotels, etc., can be obtained from the official local tourism information offices (**Turist Danışma/Turist İnformasyon**), or from travel agents and some hotel receptions (*see Unit 15*).

— Here are some common **road signs**, the symbols of which follow the international standards:
DİKKAT (caution); DUR (stop); MOTORLU TAŞIT GİREMEZ (no access for motorised vehicles); YAVAŞ (slow); YOL VER (give way); TEK YÖN (one-way); SAĞDAN GİDİNİZ (keep right); BOZUK SATIH (uneven surface); DİNLENME YERİ (rest area); ASKERİ ALAN (military area); YASAK (prohibited); HASTANE (hospital).

NB: Be extra cautious at road junctions and traffic lights as other drivers might be ignoring the rules, or the pedestrians may be crossing the road wherever they find a gap. On both the urban and the intercity roads, the main causes of accidents are: speed, faulty overtaking (**sollama**) and the constant presence of non-motorised vehicles and pedestrians on the road.

5 Public Transport

a. Railways **b.** Aeroplanes **c.** Ships
d. Public Transport **e.** Information

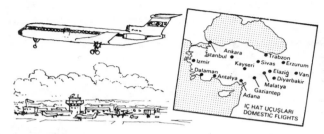

a. (Devlet) Demiryolları — *(State) Railways*
tren — *train*
istasyon/tren istasyonu/gar — *railway station*
Emanet(çi) — *Left Luggage (Office)*
Gişe/Bilet Gişesi — *Ticket Office*
bilet — *ticket*
rezervasyon/yer ayırtma — *reservation*
peron — *platform*
şehirlerarası tren — *long distance, intercity train*
Ekspres — *fast intercity train*
Pulman — *open carriages with Pullman seats*
Mavi Tren — *'Blue Train' (special express between İstanbul-Ankara)*
banliyö treni — *suburban train*
yataklı tren — *train with sleeping cars*
restoran/yemekli vagon — *Dining car*
kuşetli — *Couchettes car*
kompartman — *compartment*
Bekleme Salonu — *Waiting Room*
'OO'/Tuvalet/Hela — *WC/toilets*
hamal/taşıyıcı — *porter*

Haydarpaşa Garı	*Haydarpaşa station*
Ankara'ya birinci sınıf iki bilet lütfen.	*Two first-class tickets to Ankara, please.*
gidiş-dönüş bileti	*return ticket*
öğrenci indirimli (bilet)	*student concession (ticket)*
İki no'lu peron	*Platform 2*

b. havaalanı/hava limanı — *airport*
dış hatlar terminali — *international (air) terminal*
iç hatlar terminali — *internal (air) terminal*
uçak/uçak yolculuğu — *aeroplane/air travel*
uçuş (numarası) — *flight (number)*

c. liman — *port/harbour*
iskele — *quay/landing-place*
gemi/vapur — *boat/ship*
güverte — *deck*
kabin/kamara — *cabin*

vapur iskelesi	*boat harbour*
yat limanı	*marina*

d. otobüs/belediye otobüsü — *bus/municipal bus*
şehirlerarası otobüs — *intercity bus (coach)*
gündüz otobüsü/gece otobüsü — *day bus/night bus*
otogar — *intercity bus terminal*
troleybüs — *trolley-bus, electric bus*
otobüs durağı — *bus stop*
dolmuş (durağı) — *shared taxi (stop)*
otobüs bileti — *bus ticket*
taksi — *taxi*
Serbest (taksi) — *Free (taxi)*
(dolmuş/taksi) ücreti — *(shared taxi/taxi) fare*

Otobüs durağı nerede?	*Where is the bus stop?*
Bir bilet lütfen.	*A ticket, please.*
. . .'ye kaça götürürsünüz?	*How much is it to . . .?*
. . .'ye lütfen.	*To . . . , please.*
Sağda dururmusunuz.	*Can you stop on the right, please.*

e. Danışma — *Information/Enquiries*
tarife — *timetable/fixed taxi or dolmuş fare*

kalkış (saatı) — *departure (time)*
varış (saatı) — *arrival (time)*
rötar(lı)/gecikme(li) — *delay(ed)*

Customs→2, Times→8, Money→9

5 Public Transport

What sign do you look for:

1 if you need information?

2 if you want to leave your luggage?

3 if you want the day bus only?

4 How do you ask where the bus stop is?

5 How do you ask for a ticket to Antalya?

6 You want to go on a boat tour of the Bosphorus. Which sign tells you the way to the harbour?

7 You want to sleep on your train journey. Which carriage do you travel in?

8 You want to go to the airport. What do you say to the taxi driver?

9 What do you ask if you want to transfer from the internal air terminal to the international one?

10 How do you ask for a porter to carry your luggage?

11 You are in a dolmuş queue. Ask how much the fare to the Topkapı Palace (**Topkapı Sarayı**) is.

12 How do you ask for the ticket office?

— **Air travel:** There are airports in most major cities and near tourist centres. The service is good and frequent.

— **Trains:** Except for the İstanbul-Ankara line on which there are faster trains, trains in Turkey are generally slow and not as comfortable or as frequent as those in Western Europe. Take express trains (**Ekspres tren**) if you have to travel by rail; or the **Mavi Tren** (between İstanbul-Ankara) which is good. If you are not in a hurry, and want to mix with Turkish people, the train may be an exciting way to travel. For overnight journeys, sleepers (**yataklı tren**) are advisable.

— **Bus:** Most intercity travel in Turkey is done by buses. They cover the whole country, are frequent, very fast(!), inexpensive and generally very comfortable. They are run by private companies, and all start from intercity bus termini (**otogar**, or **şehirlerarası otobüs terminali**). For a small extra in fares, it is worth going to better companies. Ask for **lüks servis** (luxury service) and air conditioning. Book in advance at the city centre offices or at the terminus.
In cities, bus and trolley-bus services are good and cheap. In most cities, you must buy a book of tickets from special kiosks near major stops.

— **Dolmuş:** A novel means of urban public transport. 5 passengers in cars (10+ in minibuses), pay approximately 1/5 of the normal taxi fare. They are clearly marked by yellow bands, have special stops, and serve nearly all urban destinations.

— **Taxis:** Convenient and inexpensive. They have ranks and some companies have buzzers on lamp-posts that ring at the local taxi office. In most cities taxis have meters. If not, ask about the fare to your destination (. . . 'ye kaça götürürsünüz?) before getting in.

— **Boats:** In İstanbul, a crossing on the Bosphorus boats (**Boğaz Vapuru**) is convenient and cheap, and the round tour along the Bosphorus is an unforgettable experience.
There are boat services between İstanbul and Bursa, and to and from Mediterranean ports, run by State Maritime Lines (**Devlet Deniz Yolları**).

NB: There are no undergrounds in Turkish cities. Try the **Tünel** (a historic cable car) near Galata, İstanbul, for fun.

6 Accommodation

a. Hotels, Camping **b.** Hotel Rooms **c.** Prices
d. Toilets

a. otel	*hotel*
motel	*motel*
pansiyon	*guest house*
kamp/kamping	*camping*
kamp yeri	*campsite*
yurt/öğrenci yurdu	*hostel/student hostel*
gençlik yurdu	*youth hostel*

Bir otel arıyorum.	*I'm looking for a hotel.*
İyi bir otel. Çok pahalı olmasın.	*A good hotel. Not very expensive.*
Kamp yeri nerede?	*Where is the campsite?*

b. resepsiyon/müdüriyet	*reception desk/manager's office*
oda	*room*
yatak	*bed*
duş	*shower*
banyo(lu)	*(with) bathroom*
anahtar	*key*
giriş katı	*ground floor*
kat	*floor/storey*
merdiven	*stairs*
asansör	*lift*

Boş bir odanız var mı?	*Do you have a room free?*
Çift yataklı bir oda ayırtmıştım.	*I booked a double room.*
Bir gecelik bir oda (lütfen).	*A room for one night (please).*
İki yataklı bir oda.	*A room with two beds.*
Duş ve tuvaletli istiyoruz.	*We'd like one with shower and toilet.*
Otel(imiz) dolu./Otelimizde yer yok.	*The hotel is full.*
Anahtarım lütfen.	*My key, please.*
Oda numaranız kaç?	*Your room number?*
zemin kat/giriş katı	*ground floor*
birinci/ikinci kat	*first/second floor*

c. **oda ücreti/fiat**	*price*
pahalı	*expensive*
fatura	*bill*
tam/yarım pansiyon	*full/half board*

Oda ücreti ne kadar?	*How much is the room?*
Kahvaltı dahil ne kadar?	*How much is it with breakfast?*
Çok pahalı.	*It's too expensive.*
Faturayı ödeyebilirmiyim?	*Can I pay the bill now, please?*
Buyrun, faturanız.	*Here's your bill.*

d. **Tuvalet/WC/'OO' (yüz numara)**	*toilets*
Bay	*Gentlemen*
Bayan	*Ladies*
meşgul	*engaged*
boş/serbest	*vacant*
tuvalet kağıdı	*toilet roll, tissue*

Tuvaletler nerede?	*Where are the toilets?*
Şurada, solda/sağda/karşıda	*Over there, on the left/ right/across there*
Odamda/banyomda su akmıyor.	*There is no water in my room/bathroom.*

Customs→2, Parking→3, Money→9, Meals→10

6 Accommodation

What are these called in Turkish?

1   2

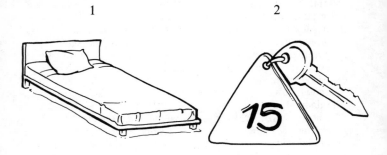

3   You're looking for a good hotel. What do you say to a passer-by?

4   How do you ask at the reception desk whether they have a vacant room?

5   You want a room with shower for one night. What do you say?

6   Ask how much the room costs with breakfast.

7   Say that you find the room too expensive.

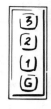

8   What is a hotel bill called in Turkish?

9   You are in the lift and want to go to the ground floor. Which button do you press?

10   You want to know where the toilets are. What do you say?

11   What does the sign say if the toilet is vacant?

12   What does it say if the toilet is engaged?

— **Hotels:** There are five grades of hotel in Turkey, first-class (**birinci sınıf**) and luxury (**lüks**) being the most comfortable. The 'star' rating system is used in most hotels; **beş-yıldızlı** five star, **dört-yıldızlı** four star. Rates are given for single or double bed rooms. Rates are usually displayed, but ask if they are not. For hotels at seaside resorts (which are usually full-board) rates may be on a weekly basis. Guest houses (**pansiyon**) usually charge for the room, rather than per person. Most receptionists in better hotels speak some English or German. All visitors are required to fill in a registration form (**kayıt**) on arrival, with details of passport, etc. Rules regarding vacating your room are the same as in other countries, but ask if in doubt (**Yarın otelden ayrılıyoruz, odayı ne zaman boşaltmamız gerekiyor?**).

— The Turkish Ministry of Culture and Tourism produces useful **hotel lists** covering most cities and resorts. For these and other information on Turkey contact:
Turkish Tourism and Information Office
170–173 Piccadilly, First Floor
London W1V 19DD
Tel. 01 734 8681–86.

— **Camping/caravanning:** There are many camping sites, especially along the coast line. Some can be booked in advance, and it is advisable to do so as places may be in great demand during the holiday period. Check with Turkish Tourism and Information Offices for lists and details. Always camp at established camp sites, and not just anywhere you find a beautiful spot. Some hotels and motels allow tents on their back gardens.

— **Youth hostels:** Information can be obtained from the International Youth Hostel handbook. Some universities open their (usually basic) student hostels to tourists during the summer months.

— **Electric voltage** is 220 V in Turkey. Two-pin plugs are used, so take an adapter with you. Power cuts and variable (usually low) voltage are common.

7 Numbers, Weights and Measures

a. Numbers **b.** Weights and Measures

a.

0 sıfır	10 on	20 yirmi
1 bir	11 onbir	21 yirmi bir
2 iki	12 oniki	22 yirmi iki
3 üç	13 onüç	23 yirmi üç
4 dört	14 ondört	30 otuz
5 beş	15 onbeş	31 otuz bir
6 altı	16 onaltı	32 otuz iki
7 yedi	17 onyedi	33 otuz üç
8 sekiz	18 onsekiz	40 kırk
9 dokuz	19 ondokuz	50 elli

60 altmış	200 ikiyüz
70 yetmiş	210 ikiyüz on
71 yetmiş bir	300 üçyüz
72 yetmiş iki	400 dörtyüz
73 yetmiş üç	500 beşyüz
80 seksen	1 000 bin
81 seksen bir	2 000 iki bin
82 seksen iki	2 010 iki bin on
90 doksan	3 000 üç bin
99 doksan dokuz	10 000 on bin
100 yüz	150 000 yüz elli bin
101 yüz bir	1 000 000 bir milyon

b.

gram	*gram*
kilo/kilogram	*kilogram*
litre	*litre*
metre	*metre*
kilometre	*kilometre*
santimetre	*centimetre*
ne kadar?	*how many/how much?*
kaç kilo/kaç metre?	*how many kilograms/how many metres?*
az/çok	*a little/a lot*
kısa/uzun	*short/long*

İkiyüz gram peynir.	200 *grams of cheese.*
Ne kadar istiyorsunuz?	*How much do you want?*
Bir kilo domates lütfen.	*A kilo of tomatoes, please.*
Buradan Göreme'ye ikiyüz elli kilometre.	250 *kms from here to Göreme.*
Biraz süt lütfen.	*A little milk please.*

Times and Dates→8

7   Numbers, Weights and Measures

Which rooms are these hotel guests staying in?

1   Onur Bilgi bey

2   Bay ve Bayan Tezel

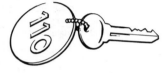

3   Sevgi hanım

4   Ms Jackson

Which bay (**peron**) do these buses leave from?

OTOBÜS TARİFESI	PERON
Antalya	5
Çeşme	8
Pamukkale	2
İzmir	1
Marmaris	3

5   The bus to Antalya.

6   The bus to Çeşme.

7   The bus to Pamukkale.

8   The bus to İzmir.

9   The bus to Marmaris.

10   Read out the following distances in Turkish:
    (a)   İstanbul–Edirne   229 km
    (b)   İstanbul–Ankara   458 km
    (c)   İstanbul–Bursa   247 km
    (d)   İstanbul–Trabzon   1078 km
    (e)   İstanbul–Bodrum   976 km
    (f)   İstanbul–Alanya   932 km

11   Where does Bay Tokman live? Read out his address in Turkish:

    Bulgur Sokak, No. 34, Daire. 7
    İstanbul

(**Sokak**: *Road*, **Daire**: *Flat*)

12   How do you ask how much a kilo of apples is?

13   How do you say you want a litre of (bottled) water?

14   You want to buy half a kilo of tomatoes. What do you say?

— In Turkey, the **metric system** of weights and measures is used:

kilo(gram)s	pounds	grams	ounces
1	= 2.2	100	= 3.5
5	= 11.0	250	= 9.0

litres	gallons	kilometres	miles
1	= .22	1	= .62
5	= 1.1	20	= 12.4

NB: 1 lb = 0.45 kg;   1 pint = 0.57 litre;
     1 gal = 4.54 litre;   1 mile = 1.6 km;   8 km = 5 miles

8 Times and Dates

a. Telling the Time **b.** Times of the Day
c. Week and Month

a. saat/kol saatı	*watch*
saat/duvar saatı	*clock*
saat	*hour*
dakika	*minute*
bir dakika	*one minute/moment*

Saat kaç?	*What's the time?*
Saat on/sabah on/akşam on.	*It's 10 o'clock (am or pm)/ 10 in the morning/10 in the evening.*
Öğleden sonra iki.	*2 in the afternoon.*
Saat on buçuk.	*It's half past 10.*
Saat onu çeyrek geçiyor.	*It's quarter past 10.*
Saat ona on var.	*It's 10 (minutes) to 10.*
Akşam altı(da).	*(At) 6 in the evening.*
Gece onbir buçuk'da.	*At half past 11 at night.*
Saat yirmiiki'de.	*(At 22 o'clock) At 10 pm.*
Saatımı kaybettim.	*I've lost my watch.*

Bir saat.	*One hour.*
Yarım saat.	*Half an hour.*
Çeyrek saat.	*Quarter of an hour.*
Bir dakika lütfen.	*Just a minute, please.*

b.

gün	*day*
sabah(leyin)	*(in the) morning*
öğle(yin)	*(at) noon*
öğleden sonra	*(in the) afternoon*
akşam	*evening*
gece	*night*
geceyarısı	*midnight*
bugün	*today*
yarın	*tomorrow*
dün	*yesterday*
hergün	*every day*

Ne zaman ayrılıyorsunuz?	*When are you leaving?*
Yarın sabah.	*Tomorrow morning.*
Bu akşam dokuz'da	*At 9 o'clock this evening.*
Tren ne zaman hareket ediyor?	*When does the train leave?*
Öğle vakti/Öğle oniki'de.	*At midday/At 12 midday.*

c.

hafta	*week*
Pazartesi	*Monday*
Salı	*Tuesday*
Çarşamba	*Wednesday*
Perşembe	*Thursday*
Cuma	*Friday*
Cumartesi	*Saturday*
Pazar	*Sunday*
hafta sonu	*weekend*
ay	*month*
yıl/sene	*year*
takvim	*calendar*

Gelecek hafta.	*Next week.*
Geçen hafta.	*Last week.*
Pazartesi'leri kapalı.	*Closed on Mondays.*
14 [Ondört] Temmuz, Salı.	*Tuesday, July 14th.*
22 [Yirmiiki] Ağustos, Perşembe.	*Thursday, August 22nd.*

Public Transport→5, Numbers→7

8 Times and Dates

1 You want to know what time it is. What do you say?

2 Say what time of the morning it is for each of the clocks below.

(a)   (b)   (c)

3 Say what time of the afternoon or evening it is.

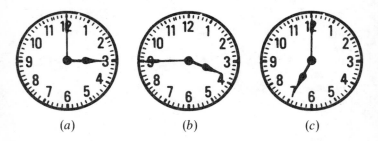

(a)   (b)   (c)

4 How do you say in Turkish:
   (a) 20 minutes;   (b) half an hour;   (c) 10 days;
   (d) 6 months?

5 Someone asks when you are leaving. Say that you are leaving at midnight.

6 You want to know what time the plane leaves. What do you say?

ARKEOLOJİ MÜZESİ

Açılış Saatleri
Pazartesi-Cuma   9 00 – 17 00
Cumartesi-Pazar   10 00 – 16 00

---

7   What are the opening times of the Arkeoloji Müzesi (Archaeological Museum)? Read them aloud.

Cumhuriyet

Sahibi: Cumhuriyet Matbaacılık ve Gaze
Nadir Nadi ● Genel Yayın Müdürü: **Has**
Uşaklıgil, Yazı İşleri Müdürü: **Okay**
Yalçın Bayer, Sayfa Düzeni Yönetme
Yalçın Doğan, İZMİR: Hikmet Çetin

TAKVİM: 21 AĞUSTOS 1988

NOKTA 30 EKİM 1988

nokta

8   When were this newspaper and this magazine published?

— The **months of the year:** Ocak, Şubat, Mart, Nisan, Mayıs, Haziran, Temmuz, Ağustos, Eylül, Ekim, Kasım, Aralık.

— **Seasons:**   **İlkbahar** Spring   **Yaz** Summer
                 Sonbahar Autumn   **Kış** Winter

— **Years:**   1989   **Bin dokuzyüz seksen dokuz**
           1990   **Bin dokuzyüz doksan**
           1991   **Bin dokuzyüz doksanbir**

— In Turkey, the **24-hour clock** is used for official purposes (e.g. on timetables, opening times, etc.) and on other occasions when the time is written down; 18.30 = 6.30 pm, and so on. There are no written equivalents of a.m. and p.m. In spoken Turkish, however, **öğleden önce** (*before noon*), **öğleden sonra** (*after noon*), **akşam** (*evening*), are used before stating the time with the 12-hour clock. For example:
Öğleden sonra birde.   At 1 in the afternoon.
Akşam dokuz onbeşte.   At 9.15 in the evening.

9 Money and Shopping

a. Money **b.** At the Bank, Changing Money
c. Shopping **d.** Paying

a. para — *money*
bozuk para — *small change*
kağıt para/banknot — *note*
madeni para — *coins*
lira/Türk lirası (TL) — *lira/Turkish lira*
cüzdan — *wallet/purse*

5000 lira lütfen.	*5000 lira, please.*
125 000 lira lütfen.	*125 000 lira, please.*

b. banka — *bank*
Kambiyo — *Exchange*
para/döviz/İngiliz sterlini — *money/foreign currency/pound sterling*
döviz değiştirmek — *to change foreign currency*
seyahat çeki — *traveller's cheque*
kredi kartı — *credit card*

50 sterlin değiştirmek istiyorum.	*I'd like to change £50.*
125 Amerikan doları.	*125 US dollars ($).*
400 Alman markı.	*400 German marks (DM).*
Kaç Türk lirası ediyor?	*How many TL does it make?*
Şu seyahat çekini değiştirmek istiyorum.	*I'd like to cash this traveller's cheque.*

c. satın almak/almak — *to buy*
dükkan/mağaza — *shop/store*
büyük mağaza — *department store*
market/bakkal — *supermarket/grocer*
pazar — *street market*
manav — *greengrocer*
self-servis — *self-service*
raf — *shelf*

Buyrun	*Welcome/May I help you?*
Ne arzu ettiniz?	*What would you like to buy?*
Bir . . . almak istiyorum.	*I'd like to buy a . . .*
Bir havlu almak istiyorum.	*I'd like to buy a towel.*
Gömlek satıyormusunuz?	*Do you sell (have) any shirts?*
Başka arzunuz (var mı)?	*Anything else?*
Çok teşekkür ederim.	*Thank you very much.*

d. fiat — *price*
ödeme/ödemek — *pay(ment)/to pay*
kasa — *cash register/cashier*
pahalı — *expensive*
ucuz — *cheap*
parasız — *free*

Bu kaça?	*How much is this?*
4500 lira.	*4500 lira.*
Çok pahalı.	*(It's) too expensive.*
Ne kadar ediyor?	*How much does that come to?*
Lütfen kasa'ya ödeyin.	*Please pay the cashier.*
Bozuk paranız var mı?	*Do you have any change?*

Numbers, Weights and Measures→7, Clothing→19

9 Money and Shopping

1 You want to change some money. What sign do you look for?

2 You enter a shop. What does the shop assistant ask you?

3 You want to know whether they have any towels. What do you say?

4 You want to know how much a shirt costs. What do you say?

5 Say that the shirt costs 22.000 TL.

6 The shop assistant asks if you would like anything else. What does she say?

7 The assistant tells you to pay at the cash desk. What does she say?

8 Ask how much it comes to.

9 Here is a receipt from a grocer in Gaziantep:
   (a) How much is the total VAT (KDV)?
   (b) What is the overall total (TOPLAM)?

```
   S.MARKET OLI-2
   ORDU C.NO:80/2-A
   TL:23035 G.ANTEP
   G.KENT   GB:1572

   27/07/1987
   FIS NO:0126
   SAAT: 19:47

   T.GID % 0 *2.938
   -----------------
   TOPKDV      *107
   TOPLAM    *3.045
   -----------------
```

10 Read out in Turkish the exchange rate for the pound (**Sterlin**): (a) Buying (**Alış**); (b) Selling (**Satış**).

DÖVİZİN CİNSİ	DÖVİZ		EFEKTİF	
T.C. ZİRAAT BANKASI 25 AĞUSTOS 1988 TARİHİNDEKİ DÖVİZ KURLARI	ALIŞ TL.	SATIŞ TL.	ALIŞ TL.	SATIŞ TL.
1 ABD DOLARI	1536.89	1539.96	1536.89	1562.94
1 AVUSTRALYA DOLARI	1255.72	1261.99	1225.75	1280.83
1 AVUSTURYA ŞİLİNİ	117.41	117.64	117.41	119.40
1 BATI ALMAN MARKI	822.30	823.94	822.30	836.24
1 BELÇİKA FRANGI	39.14	39.33	39.14	39.92
1 DANİMARKA KRONU	213.65	214.71	213.65	217.92
1 FİN MARKKASI	345.89	347.61	337.63	352.80
1 FRANSIZ FRANGI	242.08	242.56	242.08	246.18
1 HOLLANDA FLORİNİ	729.08	730.53	729.08	741.43
1 İSVEÇ KRONU	237.57	238.75	235.90	242.32
1 İSVİÇRE FRANGI	974.26	976.20	974.26	990.77
100 İTALYAN LİRETİ	110.64	111.19	107.99	112.85
1 JAPON YENİ	11.46	11.51	11.19	11.68
1 KANADA DOLARI	1242.74	1248.95	1213.07	1267.59
1 KUVEYT DİNARI	5395.42	5422.39	5266.62	5503.32
1 NORVEÇ KRONU	222.46	223.57	217.15	226.90
1 STERLİN	2598.12	2603.30	2598.12	2642.15
1 S. ARABİSTAN RİYALİ	408.72	410.76	398.96	416.89

— **Banks** are open from 9.00–12.00 and 1.00–5.00 pm, Monday to Friday. They are closed on public holidays, and sometimes earlier than usual on the afternoon before some of those holidays. (*See list of holidays in Unit 15.*)

— **Shops** are open from 9.00 am to 6.00 pm, or later. Most small supermarkets and greengrocers open much earlier and stay open well into the night. They, and the bakers, are also open on Sundays. Most towns have fruit and vegetable markets; some are daily, some are set up on certain days.

— **VAT** (KDV) is payable on most items, and the shopkeeper has to give you a receipt. Ask for it if he does not (**KDV fişini verirmisiniz**).

— Here are the names of some common shops:

bakkal/market [pronounced marcat] *grocer*	**kasap** *butcher*
manav *greengrocer*	**balıkçı** *fishmonger*
fırın/ekmekçi *baker*	**hırdavat(çı)** *hardware*
pastacı *cake shop*	**eczane** *chemist, pharmacy*
şarküteri *delicatessen*	**kitapçı** *bookshop*
kundura tamircisi *shoe repairs*	**çiçekçi** *florist*
kuyumcu *jeweller*	**gazeteci** *newsagent*
fotoğrafçı *photographer*	**şekerci** *confectioner*
kilimci *kilim rug shop*	**halıcı** *carpet shop*
antikacı *antique shop*	**kırtasiyeci** *stationery*

10 Meals

a. Meals **b.** Tableware **c.** Breakfast **d.** Snacks

<table>
<tr><td colspan="2">a.</td></tr>
<tr><td>yemek</td><td>meal/food</td></tr>
<tr><td>ye(mek)</td><td>(to) eat</td></tr>
<tr><td>yemek ye(mek)</td><td>(to) have a meal</td></tr>
<tr><td>iç(mek)</td><td>(to) drink</td></tr>
<tr><td>kahvaltı</td><td>breakfast</td></tr>
<tr><td>öğle yemeği</td><td>lunch</td></tr>
<tr><td>çay/ikindi çayı</td><td>tea/afternoon tea</td></tr>
<tr><td>akşam yemeği</td><td>dinner/supper</td></tr>
<tr><td>içecek</td><td>beverages</td></tr>
<tr><td>içki</td><td>(alcoholic) drink</td></tr>
<tr><td>yemek salonu</td><td>dining-room</td></tr>
<tr><td colspan="2">b.</td></tr>
<tr><td>fincan/kahve fincanı</td><td>cup (for Turkish coffee)</td></tr>
<tr><td>bardak</td><td>glass</td></tr>
<tr><td>şişe</td><td>bottle</td></tr>
<tr><td>kase</td><td>bowl</td></tr>
<tr><td>sürahi</td><td>jug</td></tr>
<tr><td>tabak</td><td>plate, dish</td></tr>
<tr><td>çorba tabağı</td><td>soup bowl</td></tr>
<tr><td>kaşık</td><td>spoon</td></tr>
<tr><td>çatal</td><td>fork</td></tr>
<tr><td>bıçak</td><td>knife</td></tr>
<tr><td>peçete</td><td>napkin</td></tr>
<tr><td>masa örtüsü</td><td>table cloth</td></tr>
</table>

Bir kahve lütfen.	*A (cup of) coffee, please.*
Bir şişe (beyaz/kırmızı) şarap lütfen.	*A bottle of (white/red) wine, please.*
Bir bardak su lütfen.	*A glass of water, please.*

c.

ekmek	*bread [Turkish style]*
pide	*loaf of bread/pitta bread [local]*
francala	*loaf of bread*
börek	*pie*
tereyağı	*butter*
reçel/marmelat	*jam/marmalade*
kahve	*coffee*
çay	*tea*
kakao	*hot chocolate*
meyva suyu	*fruit juice*
süt	*milk*
yoğurt	*yoghurt*

Kahve mi, çay mı?	*Coffee or tea?*
Az/orta/çok şekerli (bir) kahve lütfen.	*(A) Turkish coffee with little/ medium/plenty of sugar, please*
sütlü kahve	*coffee with milk*
limonlu çay	*tea with lemon*
çilek/vişne reçeli	*strawberry/black cherry jam*

d.

sandviç	*sandwich (made with rolls)*
tost	*toasted sandwich*
peynir(li)	*(with) cheese*
sosisli/sucuklu	*with sausage/spicy sausage*
dönerli	*with döner kebab*
omlet	*omelette*
kızarmış patates/çips	*chips/crisps*

Sandviçiniz var mı?	*Do you have any sandwiches?*
Bir sucuklu sandviç lütfen.	*A spicy sausage roll, please.*
Bir peynirli tost lütfen.	*A toasted cheese sandwich, please.*
Bir peynirli omlet lütfen.	*A cheese omelette, please.*
Bir dönerli sandviç lütfen	*A 'döner' sandwich please.*

Paying→9, Restaurants→11, Drinking→14

10 Meals

1 What are the three meals of the day called in Turkish?

2 What are the following called in Turkish?

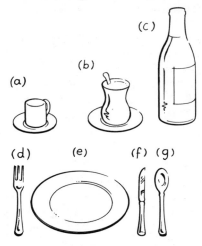

3 What is being served on the tray?

4 You'd like a glass of white wine. What do you say to the waiter?

5 How would you ask for some bread?

6 You want two cups of Turkish coffee with medium sugar. What do you ask for?

7 Say that you would like a cheese omelette.

8 How would you ask for two döner sandwiches?

— **Meals:** Turkish breakfast (**kahvaltı**) consists of slices of fresh local bread, Turkish tea in small glasses (no milk), cheese, black olives, marmalade and margarine or butter (except in new tourist hotels where a more international menu is served). In some areas lentil soup and fresh bread, or crisp ring-shaped sesame breadcake (**simit**) accompanied by fetta cheese (**beyaz peynir**) and melon (**kavun**) with tea is a common way of starting the day. Lunch is the main meal in most areas. Some shops may be closed for lunch. Eating out in road-side or open-air restaurants is a popular and enjoyable activity during the summer. Also popular for a quick snack-lunch are sandwiches, cheese or meat pastry (**börek**), cold yoghurt drink (**ayran**) or fruit juice, followed by milk pudding (**muhallebi**, **kazan dibi**) or sweet pastry (**baklava**). Most snack bars (**sandviççi**), patisseries (**pastacı**) and restaurants are open long hours. Turkish food is very rich and varied, using all varieties of vegetables and lamb or beef.

— Some useful words and expressions:
acı(lı) *spicy*   **Acılı olmasın.** *Not spicy, please.*
yağlı *fatty/oily*   **Yağsız olsun.** *Not fatty, please.*
soğuk/sıcak *cold/hot*   **Biraz buz lütfen.** *Some ice, please.*

— It is customary to say **afiyet olsun** (good appetite) to others having a meal, or after the meal.

a. Restaurants **b.** Service, Menu **c.** Seasonings
d. The Bill

a. lokanta/restoran	*restaurant*
meyhane	*pub serving food (usually for men)*
birahane	*beer bar*
kahve(hane)/çayhane	*traditional Turkish café*
masa	*table*
sandalye	*chair*
teras/bahçe	*terrace/garden*

Yemek yemek istiyoruz.	*We'd like to eat.*
Kaç kişisiniz?	*How many persons?*
Üç kişilik bir masanız var mı?	*Do you have a table for 3?*
Boş bir masanız var.	*There's a free table.*

b.

menü/yemek listesi	*menu*
yemeği ısmarla(mak)	*(to) order food*
servis	*course/table service*
fiks menü	*fixed menu/set meal*
meze	*snack with drinks/appetiser*
tatlı	*dessert*
meyva	*fruit*
peynir	*cheese*
içki listesi	*drinks list (wine list)*

Menüyü rica edebilirmiyiz?	*Could we have the menu, please?*
İki şiş kebap lütfen.	*Two skewered kebabs, please.*
Tatlı ne arzu edersiniz?	*What would you like for dessert?*
Ne içersiniz?	*What would you like to drink?*
Kahve istermisiniz?	*Would you like some coffee?*

c.

şeker	*sugar*
tuz	*salt*
kara biber	*black pepper*
kırmızı biber	*hot paprika*
yağ/zeytin yağı	*oil/olive oil*
sirke	*vinegar*
kürdan	*tooth-pick*

d.

garson	*waiter*
hesap	*bill*
servis dahil (değildir)	*service (not) included*
bahşiş	*tip*

Garson!	*Waiter!*
Hesabı (getirirmisiniz) lütfen!	*(Bring me) the bill, please!*
Üstü kalsın.	*Keep the change.*

Toilets→6, Paying→10, Drinking→14

11   Restaurants

1   Where do you go:
    (a) to have coffee and a cake?
    (b) to have lunch or dinner?
    (c) to have a drink?

2   You want to ask if a table is
    free. What do you say?

3   Tell the waiter you'd
    like something to eat.

4   Tell the waiter you'd
    like the menu.

5   You would like to have the
    salt. What do you say?

6   After you've ordered your food, the waiter asks what you'd
    like to drink. What does he say?

7   After the meal you'd like to pay. What do you say to the
    waiter?

8   You want to ask if service is included. What do you say?

9   The waiter wants to give you back the change, but you
    want him to keep it as a tip. What do you say?

10 What are these called in Turkish?

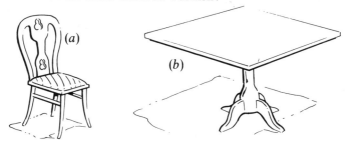

(a)

(b)

11 What are the following called in Turkish?

— Here are some of the many types of **restaurants** in Turkey:

Lokanta	*mixed menu*
Kebapçı	*kebab house/meat dishes only*
Pideci	*Turkish pizza, pie*
Tatlıcı/Baklavacı	*traditional sweets and puddings*
Pastacı	*pastry shop (also ice cream, cold beverages, puddings)*
Kafeterya	*self-service*

— Most restaurants offer good quality food at reasonable prices. They usually display their range near the window, and do not object to customers who want to see what's in the kitchen. The self-service ones tend to be less traditional. In traditional restaurants you can order by pointing to the dish you want. Some do not serve alcoholic drinks.

— It is usual to leave a tip (**bahşiş**) of about 10% for the waiter.

— Unless it is a formal meal or dinner, you may try having your dessert after your meal at a **tatlıcı** (or **baklavacı**) where better quality and variety may be available.

12 Starters, Meat, Fish

a. Starters **b.** Meat **c.** Poultry, Eggs **d.** Fish

a. çorba — *soup*
    et suyu çorbası — *clear soup, consommé*
    söğüş salata/çoban salatası — *tomato and cucumber salad*
    karışık salata — *mixed vegetable salad*
    yoğurt — *plain yoghurt (with main course)*
    cacık — *cucumber and yoghurt with mint*

---

    mercimek çorbası — *lentil soup*
    domatesli pirinç çorbası — *tomato and rice soup*
    sebze çorbası — *vegetable soup*
    şehriye çorbası — *noodle soup*
    yoğurtlu çorba — *yoghurt soup (with rice and mint)*

    yalancı dolma/sarma — *stuffed pepper or vine leaves*
    dolma — *stuffed aubergines, pepper, etc.*

    imam bayıldı — *aubergine salad*

---

b. Et — *Meat*
    sığır (eti) — *beef*
    dana (eti) — *veal*
    koyun/kuzu (eti) — *lamb*
    siyah et — *red meat*
    biftek — *beef steak*
    pirzola — *chop*
    domuz eti — *ham, pork [not eaten in Turkey]*

Kebap	*kebab: various types of grilled meat*
Şiş kebap/kuşbaşı kebap	*skewered meat cubes*
Döner kebap	*meat roasted on a vertical spit*
Izgara köfte	*grilled meat balls*
Salçalı köfte/İzmir köftesi	*meat balls or croquettes in tomato sauce/in gravy*
Lahmacun	*Turkish meat pizza, spicy, with vegetables*

Kebabınız nasıl olsun?	*How do you like your kebab?*
Az/orta/iyi pişmiş, lütfen.	*Rare/medium/well done, please*
Yanında pilav olsun lütfen.	*I'd like some rice with it, please.*

c. Kümes hayvanları — *Poultry*
- **tavuk** — *chicken*
- **hindi** — *turkey*
- **ördek** — *duck*
- **yumurta** — *egg*

tavuk ızgara	*roast chicken*
tavuklu pilav	*chicken rice*
omlet	*omelette*

d. Balık — *Fish*
- **dil balığı** — *sole*
- **alabalık** — *trout*
- **uskumru** — *mackerel*
- **barbunya** — *red mullet*
- **kalkan** — *turbot*
- **levrek** — *sea bass*
- **palamut** — *tuna*
- **morina** — *cod*
- **midye/midye tavası** — *mussels/sautéed mussels*
- **istakoz** — *lobster*
- **karides** — *prawns/shrimps*
- **istiridye** — *oyster*

What do you say to the waiter:

1   If you want vegetable soup?

2   If you want stuffed vine leaves?

3   If you want skewered cubes of meat?

4   If you want your kebab well done?

5   If you want rice with your kebab?

6   If you want a cheese omelette?

7   If you want chicken rice?

8   What are these dishes called:

9   Try to translate into English the names of the ingredients (**malzeme**) which are being used in the recipe below:

BAHÇE KEBABI

MALZEME:
Yarım kilo koyun eti şişlik kuşbaşı, 1 tane patlıcan, 1 tane sert domates, 2 tane yeşil biber (dolmalık), 1 tane soğan, 2 çorba kaşığı sade yağ, karabiber, tuz.

— Lunch and dinner at Turkish restaurants start with soup or salad, white cheese and hot bread (**pide**). If you are going to have a leisurely dinner with drinks, other starters such as **yalancı dolma, tarama salatası, imam bayıldı, hummus**, etc. are recommended. The main meat or vegetable-based course is served with bread, salad and/or rice. The last course is desserts, sweets or fruit, followed by Turkish coffee. (*See also Units 11 and 13.*)

— Some useful words:

kızarmış/tavada *fried*	**ızgara** *grilled*
rosto *roasted*	**fırında/tandır** *baked*
şiş *skewered*	**zeytinyağlı** *cooked in olive oil*
haşlanmış/haşlama *boiled/ stewed*	

13 Vegetables, Fruit, Desserts

a. Vegetables **b.** Fruit **c.** Desserts, Sweets

TURKISH DELIGHT

a. Sebze	*Vegetable(s)*
patates	*potatoes*
patates kızarmiş/çips	*chips/crisps*
havuç	*carrots*
bezelye	*peas*
domates	*tomatoes*
yeşil fasulye	*runner beans*
enginar	*artichoke*
soğan	*onion*
sarımsak	*garlic*
lahana	*cabbage*
mantar	*mushroom*
salatalık/hıyar	*cucumber*
marul/yeşil salata	*lettuce*
biber	*green or red pepper*
ıspanak	*spinach*
patlıcan	*aubergine/eggplant*
kabak	*courgette/marrow*
bamya	*ladies' fingers/okra*
nohut	*chick-peas*
mercimek	*lentils*
kuru fasulye	*beans*
pirinç	*rice (uncooked)*
(pirinç) pilav	*rice (cooked)*
zeytin	*olives*

türlü	*mixed vegetable stew*
etli fasulye	*runner bean stew*
dolma	*stuffed vegetables*
etli nohut	*chick-pea stew*
kuru fasulye	*bean stew*
karnıyarık	*aubergine stuffed with mince meat*

b. Meyva — *Fruits*

elma	*apples*
armut	*pears*
limon	*lemon*
vişne	*cherries*
çilek	*strawberries*
portakal	*orange*
incir	*figs*
kavun	*melon*
karpuz	*water melon*
şeftali	*peaches*
üzüm	*grapes*
kaysı	*apricots*
muz	*bananas*
antep fıstığı	*pistachio nuts*
fındık	*hazel nuts*

hoşaf/komposto	*compote*
çekirdeksiz üzüm	*seedless grapes*
Yarım kilo incir lütfen.	*Half a kilo of figs, please.*
Ben şeftaliyi severim.	*I like peaches.*

c. Tatlı — *Sweets/Desserts*

dondurma	*ice cream*
hamur tatlısı	*sweet pastry*
baklava	*baklava (sweet flaky pastry filled with nuts)*
lokum (sade/fıstıklı)	*Turkish Delight (plain/pistachio)*
muhallebi/sütlaç/keşkül	*milk, rice or almond puddings*
kazandibi	*caramelised milk pudding*
pasta/kek	*cake/dry cake*

13   Vegetables, Fruit, Desserts

çikolata	*chocolate*
krema	*cream*

Bir porsiyon fıstıklı baklava.	*One portion of pistachio baklava.*
Bir vişneli dondurma lütfen.	*Some cherry ice cream, please.*
Bir dondurmalı kazandibi.	*One kazandibi with ice cream.*

What are the following in Turkish? Say you like them/don't like them.

Start: **Ben . . . -i** (or -ı, -u, -ü, -yi, etc.) **severim.** (I like . . .)

   Ben . . . -i sevmem. (I don't like . . .)

Example: Ben kuru fasulyeyi severim.

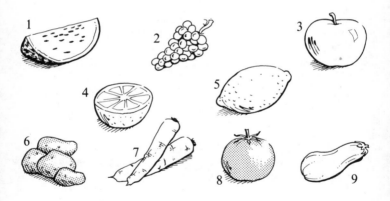

10   Say you would like to buy some Turkish Delight.

11   Ask the waiter to bring you some baklava.

12   You would like an ice cream. What sign do you look for?

13   You would like ice cream with your kazandibi. What do you ask the waiter?

14   What is the sweet pastry with nuts called?

— Rice (**pilav**) is one of the staple foods in Turkey. As with salads, **sade pilav** (plain boiled rice with butter) is served with the main dish. There are richer varieties of rice, such as **iç pilav** or **meyhane pilavı** (rice with meat, nuts and currants). In Anatolia, **bulgur pilavı** (cracked wheat pilav) is very popular.

— In Turkey, **salads** are usually served either as a starter or with the main dish – sometimes on the same plate. You can always order additional side salads. Varieties include: **karışık salata, söğüş, piyaz, çoban salatası, cacık, Rus salatası.**

— **Bread** and **bottled water** are served with almost every meal. (Of course, you do not have to eat or drink them!)

— For **vegetarians** there are many, generally cold, dishes in most restaurants, especially starters, and most dishes cooked in olive oil are without meat. **Peynirli börek, sigara böreği, yalancı dolma** (all ordered with salad) or **piyaz** can form tasty and filling meals. **Pideci** (Turkish pizza restaurants) also have varieties without meat.

— **Social eating:** If a Turkish family invites you for a meal, you do not normally 'take a bottle' – unless you are sure that they drink alcohol. But a box of sweets or some flowers would be well received (they do not usually open the box when you are there). Eating habits and table manners vary considerably, but meals are usually shorter than in Britain, guests are generally offered more food than they can consume, and coffee (or tea) is usually served later, in the living room.

— The vocabulary in Units 11, 12 and 13 has covered many of the items to be found on a Turkish menu, and will help you in choosing dishes in a restaurant. In tourist resorts the menus may be printed in Turkish and English. But you can also ask to see the food before you order (**Lütfen yemekleri görebilir-miyim? Can I see the dishes please?**).

14 Drinking and Smoking

a. Non-alcoholic Drinks **b.** Alcoholic Drinks
c. Smoking

a. içecek/meşrubat	*beverages/refreshments*
şişe suyu	*bottled drinking water*
maden suyu/soda	*mineral water/soda water*
meyva suyu	*fruit juice*
limonata	*lemonade*
gazoz	*carbonated sugary drinks*
ayran	*diluted natural yoghurt drink*
kahve/Türk kahvesi	*Turkish coffee*
sade, acı/az şekerli/orta şekerli	*without sugar/little sugar/ medium sweet*
neskafe	*instant coffee*
çay	*tea*
süt	*milk*
pastorize/uzun ömürlü (UHT)	*pasteurised/long life*

Susadım.	*I'm thirsty.*
Bir şişe suyu lütfen.	*A bottle of drinking water, please.*
Bir vişne suyu lütfen.	*A cherry juice, please.*
Orta şekerli bir kahve.	*A medium sweet Turkish coffee.*
Bir çay daha lütfen.	*Another tea, please.*
Süt te alabilirmiyim?	*Can I have some milk too?*

b. bira *beer*
  fıçı birası *draught beer*
  şarap (beyaz/kırmızı) *wine (white/red)*
  rakı *anisette (high alcohol drink with aniseed)*
  votka *vodka*
  cin/tonik *gin/tonic water*
  konyak *cognac*
  şişe *bottle*
  şişe açacağı/tirbışon *bottle opener*
  sek/tatlı *dry/sweet*
  beyaz/kırmızı/pembe *white/red/rosé*
  köpüklü *sparkling*
  soğuk/oda sıcaklığında *chilled/at room temperature*

Bir soğuk bira lütfen.	*A cold beer, please.*
Bir şişe . . .	*A bottle of . . .*
Bir bardak . . .	*A glass of . . .*
Bir küçük şişe iyi beyaz şarap.	*A small bottle of good white wine.*
Bir bardak kırmızı şarap.	*A glass of red wine.*
Biraz buz lütfen.	*Some ice, please.*
Şerefe!	*Cheers!*

c. sigara *cigarette*
  filtreli sigara *filter cigarette*
  püro *cigar*
  pipo tütünü *pipe tobacco*
  kibrit/çakmak *matches/lighter*
  kül tablası *ashtray*

Sigara İçilmez!/Sigara içmek yasaktır!	*No smoking/Smoking is forbidden!*
Burada sigara içebilirmiyim?	*Can I smoke here?*
Dumanınız beni rahatsız ediyor.	*Your smoke is disturbing me.*
Bir paket . . . lütfen.	*A packet of . . . (brand) . . . , please.*
Bir kutu kibrit lütfen.	*A box of matches, please.*
Bir sigara alırmısınız?	*Would you like a cigarette?*
Teşekkür ederim, içmiyorum.	*No thank you, I don't smoke.*

Meals→10

14 Drinking and Smoking

1   The waiter asks if you would like coffee or tea. What does he say?

2   Ask for two medium sweet Turkish coffees.

3   How do you ask for a packet of cigarettes and a box of matches?

4   What do you say if you want some ice?

What are these called in Turkish?

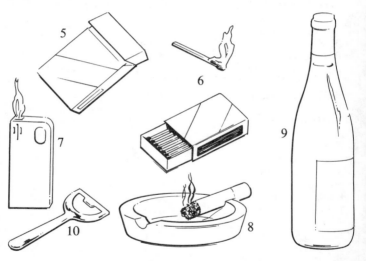

You have ordered a meal. The waiter asks if you would like anything to drink: **Ne içersiniz?** (or **İçecek birşey istermisiniz?**). Say you would like the items below.
Start: **Bir . . . lütfen.** (A . . . , please).

11   some diluted yoghurt drink

12   a bottle of red wine

13   a cold beer

14   a bottle of mineral water.

— Turkish people drink bottled water, **ayran**, cola, fresh or bottled fruit juices, beer, rakı or wine with their food depending on the occasion and whether it is a family meal or, say, a men-only drinking party. Rakı (a high alcohol spirit distilled from grapes and flavoured with aniseed) is a 'national' drink, especially for men. Wine is not expensive, so order or buy the better ones. Beer (mainly lager) is good.

— Turkish coffee (**kahve**) is always served black. It is strong and not filtered, so the sediment is left in the cup. Specify the desired amount of sugar while ordering – sugar is added while making it.

— Tea (**çay**) is the most popular refreshment, but never served with milk. It is generally brewed in double kettles or samovars, and served in small glasses.

— Coffee houses (**kahve** or **kahvehane**) perform a function similar to pubs, but mostly serve beverages and no food. They are traditionally for men, except those in tourist resorts.

— **Water:** Try to drink only bottled water (**şişe suyu**).

15 Sightseeing and Entertainment

a. Tourism **b.** Places of Interest
c. Entertainment **d.** Admission

a.

turist	tourist
Turizm Danışma	*Tourist Information Office*
bilgi	*information*
broşür	*brochure*
harita	*map*
seyahat acentası	*travel agency*

Turizm Danışma nerede?	*Where is the Tourist Information Office?*
. . . hakkında bilgi istiyorum.	*I'd like some information on . . .*
İngilizce biliyormusunuz?	*Do you speak English?*

b.

görülecek yerler	sights
tarihi yerler	*historic places/sights*
müze	*museum*
sergi	*exhibition*
saray	*palace*
cami	*mosque*
kilise	*church*
tapınak	*temple*
anıt	*monument*
bina	*building*
kapalı çarşı	*covered bazaar*
sanat (eserleri)	*(works of) art*
mimarlık (eserleri)	*(works of) architecture*
Osmanlı	*Ottoman*

eski şehir	*old city*
kale/surlar	*castle, citadel/fortifications*
harabe(ler)	*ruin(s)*
hamam	*Turkish bath*
kaplıca	*spa*
türbe	*tomb*

Topkapı Sarayı	*Topkapı Palace*
Ayasofya ve Sultan Ahmet	*Santa Sophia and the Blue Mosque*
Süleymaniye Camiine nasıl gidilir?	*Which way is it to the Süleymaniye Mosque?*

c. tiyatro	*theatre*
sinema	*cinema*
folklor dansları	*folk dancing*
gece kulübü/gazino	*night club*
konser salonu	*concert hall*
festival	*festival*
stadyum	*stadium*

İstanbul Festivali programı var mı?	*Do you have the programme for the İstanbul Festival?*
İyi bir gece kulübü tavsiye edermisiniz?	*Can you recommend a good night club?*

d. açılış saatleri	*opening hours*
açık	*open*
kapalı	*closed*
giriş	*entrance*
çıkış	*exit*
Girilmez!/Girmek yasaktır!	*No entry!/No trespassing!*
gişe	*cashier/ticket office*
bilet	*ticket*
ücret	*price/fare/fee*
itiniz/çekiniz	*push/pull*
rehber	*tourist guide*
ziyaret/tur	*visit/tour*

Biletiniz lütfen!	*Your ticket, please.*
Şehir turları nereden (ne zaman) başlıyor?	*Where (When) do the city tours start?*

15 Sightseeing and Entertainment

Do you know these tourist attractions in Turkey? Can you name them?

5 You'd like advice on reserving a hotel room and brochures on places of interest. Where can you find help?

6 You're going on a tour of the city. Your friend asks what time the tour starts. What does he say?

7 Tell him that it starts at seven o'clock.

You're visiting a museum. Which sign do you look for

8 to find out the opening times?

9 when you want to buy admission tickets?

10 Which sign indicates the entrance?

11 Which sign indicates the exit?

12 The museum, the shop or the garage are closed. What does the sign say?

— There are **Turizm Danışma** (Tourist Information) offices in most cities and holiday resorts, e.g. Atatürk Airport, İstanbul; Meşrutiyet Cad. 57/B, Galatasaray, İstanbul, Tel. 145 68 75; Gazi Mustafa Kemal Bul. 33, Ankara, Tel. 129 29 30; Atatürk Cad. 418, Alsancak, İzmir, Tel. 21 68 41.

— For **motorists** there are the offices of Turing ve Otomobil Kulübü (Touring and Automobile Club); in İstanbul (Halaskargazi Cad. 364, Şişli, Tel. 146 70 90); İzmir (Atatürk Bul. 370, Alsancak, Tel. 12 20 92).

— A few of the most important museums (**müzeler**) and historic sights in Turkey include the following.

— **In İstanbul:** Topkapı Sarayı (The Ottoman Palace complex). Arkeoloji Müzesi (Museum of Antiquities). Şark Eserleri Müzesi (Museum of Oriental Antiquities). Resim ve Heykel Müzesi (Museum of Turkish Painting and Sculpture). *Churches*: Ayasofya Camii (St. Sophia, previously a mosque, now a museum), Aya İrini, St Saviour. *Mosques*: Süleymaniye Camii, Sultan Ahmet Camii (Blue Mosque), Beyazıt Camii. Kapalı Çarşı (Covered Bazaar), aqueducts, Sinan Hamamı (Turkish Bath by Sinan). Boğaziçi (Bosphorus) boat trip recommended.

— **Elsewhere:** In Ankara: Etnoğrafya Müzesi (Ethnographic Museum), Anadolu Medeniyetleri Müzesi (Museum of Anatolian Civilizations), Ankara Kalesi (Ankara Citadel), Ogüst Mabedi (Temple of Augustus). In Aegean region: Efes (Efesus), Didim (Didyma), Bergama, Pamukkale, Aphrodisias. In Central Anatolia: Göreme and Ihlara ('Cappadocia' – rock-cut settlements and churches). In Edirne: Selimiye Mosque. In Mediterranean region: Patara, Side, Aspendos. Also Bursa.

— **Festivals and public holidays** (Bayram ve resmi tatiller): January 1, New Year's Day (Yılbaşı). April 23, National Sovereignty and Children's Festival (Eğemenlik ve Çocuk Bayramı). May 19, Youth and Sports Festival (Gençlik ve Spor Bayramı). August 30, Victory Festival (Zafer Bayramı). October 29, Republic Festival (Cumhuriyet Bayramı). All public offices, schools, banks and most shops close on these days. Additionally, they may close early the day before.

— There are also two Muslim Festivals (**dini bayramlar**). Ramadan (Ramazan/Şeker Bayramı) lasts three days, and the Sacrifice Festival (Kurban Bayramı) four days. Every year they fall 10 or 11 days earlier. All offices, banks and schools as well as shops close during these holidays. Many Turkish people take extended holidays during these festivals, and especially if they fall in spring or summer months, transport facilities and holiday accommodation may be overbooked.

16 Excursions and Recreation

a. Excursions **b.** Scenery **c.** Sports
d. Photography

a. tur/gezi — *excursion, outing*
görülecek yerler — *places of interest, scenic places*
manzara — *scenery*

Nerede turlarınız var?	*Where do your tours go to?*
Turlar ne kadar acaba?	*How much are the tours?*
Hareket/Dönüş ne zaman?	*What time does it leave/ return?*
İngilizce rehber var mı?	*Is there an English-speaking guide?*

b. deniz — *sea*
kıyı/sahil — *coast, sea-shore*
körfez — *bay, gulf*
yarımada — *peninsula*
ada — *island*
göl — *lake*
nehir/ırmak — *river*
orman — *forest*
koru(luk) — *wood*
park/bahçe — *park/garden(s)*
kaya(lık) — *rock(y)*
dağ(lık) — *mountain(ous)*
mağara — *cave*
sahil yolu — *coast road*

Akdeniz/Karadeniz	Mediterranean/Black Sea
Ege Denizi/Marmara Denizi	Aegean Sea/Marmara Sea
Boğaziçi/İstanbul Boğazı	Bosphorus

c.

plaj	beach
kum/kumluk (plaj)	sand/sandy (beach)
yüzme havuzu	swimming pool
yüz(mek)	(to) swim
güneş/gölge	sun/shade
güneşte yan(mak)	(to) tan
şemsiye	umbrella
duş	shower
deniz yatağı	air mattress
şezlong	deck-chair
deniz motoru	motor-boat
yelkenli	sailing-boat
tenis	tennis
yürüyüş/yürüyüşe çıkmak	walk, stroll/to go for a walk
dağcılık	mountaineering

Yüzme biliyorum/bilmiyorum	I can/cannot swim
Burada yüzebilirmiyiz?	Can we swim here?
Burası derin mi?	Is it deep here?
Denize Girilmez!	No bathing!/No swimming!
Dikkat, Tehlike!	Caution, Danger!
Derin su!	Deep water!

d.

fotoğraf makinası/kamera	camera
fotoğraf (çekmek)	(to take) photograph
siyah-beyaz filim	black & white film
renkli filim/slayt filmi	colour film/slide film
filaş	flash
pil	battery
video bandı	video tape
sinema filmi (sekiz milimetrelik)	cine film (8 mm)

Renkli filim var mı?	Do you have colour film?
Otuzaltılık istiyorum.	I want a 36-exposure film.
Burada fotoğraf çekilir mi?	Is photography allowed here?
Fotoğrafınızı çekebilirmiyim?	Can I take your photograph?

16 Excursions and Recreation

What can you see in these pictures? Answer in Turkish, . . . 'i
görüyorum. For example: **Kaleyi görüyorum** (I see the citadel).

4 What sign do you look for if you want to go to:
   (a) the beach;
   (b) the swimming pool?

Say you would like to hire the following items. Ask for them in
Turkish, for example: **Bir . . . kiralamak istiyorum**.

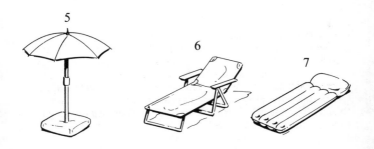

Say you would like to buy the following items. Ask for them in Turkish, for example: **Bir . . . almak istiyorum**.

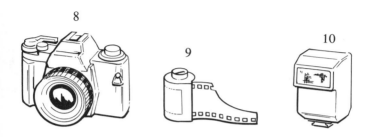

8

9

10

— Apart from İstanbul (a must for any visitor) there are various **'tourist areas'** in Turkey: the whole of the Aegean and Mediterranean coasts, historic sites on those coasts and inland, Central or Southern Anatolia (especially Cappadocia), parts of the Black Sea coast, several mountains, etc.

— **Beaches:** Several thousand miles of Aegean, Mediterranean, Marmara and Black Sea coasts provide all types of beaches. Topless sunbathing or swimming is tolerated, but check first so as not to cause offence to local customs.

— You are allowed to visit **mosques** except during prayer times. You must take your shoes off before you go in, and women must wear scarfs.

— **Photography** is allowed everywhere except near military installations, airfields, etc. It is also courteous to ask permission before taking pictures of people, especially women (**Fotoğrafınızı çekebilirmiyim?** May I take your photo?), and in rural areas. In museums and archaeological sites photography is either not allowed or you may have to buy a separate ticket. Check whether you can use a flash gun or a tripod.

17 The Weather

a. The Weather **b.** Good Weather
c. Bad Weather **d.** Cold Weather

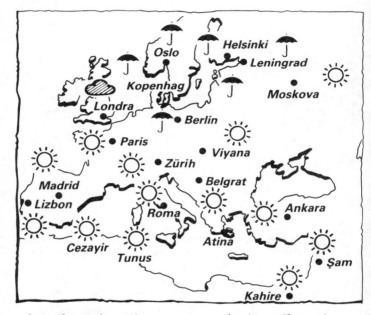

a. hava (durumu/raporu)	*weather (report/forecast)*
hava sıcaklığı	*temperature*
derece (Santigrad)	*degree (Centigrade)*

Hava nasıl?	*How is the weather?*
Hava bugün nasıl olacakmış?	*What is the weather going to be like today?*
. . .'da hava nasıl?	*How is the weather in . . .?*

b. iyi hava	*good weather*
güneş(li)	*sun(ny)*
açık hava	*clear sky*
sıcak/ılık	*hot, warm/warmish*
fena değil	*fair, not bad*
yüksek basınç	*high pressure*

Hava (çok) güzel	*The weather is (very) fine.*
Biraz sıcak	*Rather hot/hot*
Hava ne kadar güzel!	*What lovely weather!*
Deniz suyu çok sıcak.	*The sea water is very warm.*

c.

alçak basınç	*low-pressure (area)*
kötü hava	*bad weather*
bulut(lu)	*cloud(y)*
az bulutlu	*overcast*
sis(li)	*fog(gy)*
kapalı/puslu	*overcast/hazy*
yağmur(lu)/yağış	*rain(y)/rain*
sağanak yağış	*shower*
rüzgar(lı)	*wind(y)*
fırtına(lı)	*storm(y)*
sakin (hava/deniz)	*calm (weather/sea)*
dalgalı	*rough*
şemsiye	*umbrella*

Yağmur yağıyor.	*It is raining.*
Hava çok bulutlu.	*It is very cloudy.*
Yağmur yağacak.	*It's going to rain.*
Deniz çok dalgalı.	*The sea is very rough.*
Hava aşırı sıcak.	*It's excessively hot.*
Hava iyileşecek mi?	*Is the weather going to improve?*
Hava açılıyor.	*It is clearing up.*

d.

soğuk	*cold*
serin	*cool*
kar	*snow*
dolu	*hail*
don	*frost*

Çok soğuk	*Very cold*
Kar yağıyor.	*It's snowing.*
Yollarda don var mı?	*Is there ice on the roads?*
Hava sisli mi?	*Is it foggy?*

17   The Weather

Look at this weather map of Turkey from a newspaper.

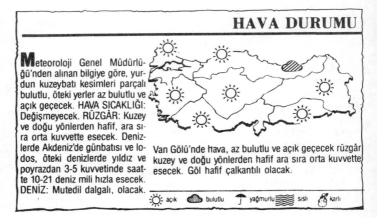

HAVA DURUMU

Meteoroloji Genel Müdürlüğü'nden alınan bilgiye göre, yurdun kuzeybatı kesimleri parçalı bulutlu, öteki yerler az bulutlu ve açık geçecek. HAVA SICAKLIĞI: Değişmeyecek. RÜZGÂR: Kuzey ve doğu yönlerden hafif, ara sıra orta kuvvette esecek. Denizlerde Akdeniz'de günbatısı ve lodos, öteki denizlerde yıldız ve poyrazdan 3-5 kuvvetinde saatte 10-21 deniz mili hızla esecek. DENİZ: Mutedil dalgalı, olacak.

Van Gölü'nde hava, az bulutlu ve açık geçecek rüzgâr kuzey ve doğu yönlerden hafif ara sıra orta kuvvette esecek. Göl hafif çalkantılı olacak.

açık   bulutlu   yağmurlu   sisli   karlı

1   What is the weather like in the Aegean region?

2   What is the weather like on the Black Sea coast?

3   What is the weather like in Eastern Turkey?

What is the weather like?

— In Turkey, temperatures are given in **Derece**, or **Santigrad** (Centigrade, Celsius). To convert them into Fahrenheit, multiply by 1.8 (or 9/5) and add 32.

Celsius	−5	0	5	10	15	20	25	30	35
Fahrenheit	23	32	41	50	59	68	77	86	95

— Newspapers as well as radio and TV (TRT) give regular weather forecasts.

18 Post Office and Telephone

a. Post Office **b.** Letters and Postcards
c. Telephone **d.** Telegram

a. posta	*post, mail*
Postahane/'PTT' [pronounced *pe-te-te*]	*Post Office/Post, Telegraph, Telephone (office)*
gişe	*counter*
posta kutusu	*letterbox*

Affedersiniz, Postahane (PTT) nerede acaba?	*Excuse me, where is the Post Office?*
PTT ne zaman açılır/kapanır?	*When does the Post Office open/close?*

b. mektup	*letter*
kart, kart-postal	*postcard*
zarf	*envelope*
adres	*address*
pul(u)	*stamp(s)*
damga(lamak)	*(to) stamp*
hatıra pulu	*commemorative stamps*
paket, koli	*parcel*
uçakla	*airmail*
adi posta	*surface mail*
taahhütlü	*registered mail*
gönderen	*sender*
alıcı	*addressee*

İngiltere'ye kart-postal kaça gider?	*How much is a post-card to Britain?*
Altı tane lütfen.	*6 of those, please.*
Şu mektubu yollamak istiyorum.	*I'd like to post this letter.*

c. telefon — *telephone*
telefon numarası — *telephone number*
telefon rehberi — *telephone directory*
telefon kulübesi — *telephone box*
numarayı çevir(mek) — *(to) dial the number*
uluslararası — *international*
santral — *operator*
hatlar (meşgul) — *lines (are busy)*
jeton — *(telephone) token*
telefon kartı — *phone card*
ödemeli — *reverse charge call*

İngiltere'ye nasıl telefon edebilirim acaba?	*Could you tell me how I can call Britain?*
Telefonunuzu kullanabilirmiyim?	*Can I use your phone?*
Numaranız kaç?	*What's your number?*
125 16 03 mü?	*Is that 125 16 03?*
Alo, ben . . . !	*Hello, this is . . . speaking!*
. . . ile görüşebilirmiyim?	*May I speak to . . . ?*
Bir dakika lütfen./Ayrılmayın.	*One moment, please./Hold the line.*
Bir not bırakabilirmiyim?	*Can I leave a message?*

d. telgraf — *telegram*
normal/acele/yıldırım — *ordinary/urgent/very urgent*
telex — *telex*
fax — *fax*
makbuz — *receipt*

İngiltere'ye bir telgraf yollamak istiyorum.	*I want to send a telegram to Britain.*
Kelimesi ne kadar?	*How much is it per word?*
Tamamı ne tutar?	*How much would it come to?*

What are these called in Turkish?

7 You want to buy a stamp for a postcard to Australia. What do you ask for?

8 How do you ask for three stamps at 400 lira each?

9 You would like someone's telephone number. What do you ask him?

10 You telephone your friend Gül. When she answers the phone, what does she say?

11 What is this called in Turkish?

12 You are not sure if you have the right number. What do you say?

— PTT, the **post office**, is distinguished by its yellow sign. Main post offices are open from 8.00–24.00 Mon.–Sat., and 9.00–19.00 Sun. Sub-post offices may close at lunch time.

— **Letterboxes** are yellow. Their opening times may vary, so for urgent mail, post at the PTT.

— **Telephones:** There are yellow telephone boxes everywhere. They do not accept coins so you must buy **jeton** (tokens) from PTT. Buy **büyük jeton** (large tokens) for international calls and keep a few spare ones. There are also card phones in most places. You can also make operator-connected calls at PTTs, but there may be queues. Directory enquiries (**Bilinmeyen numaralar**): 011.

— To make an **international telephone call:**
1. Lift receiver, wait for tone; 2. Insert jeton(s) or phonecard; 3. Dial 9 and wait for continuous dialling tone; 4. Dial 9 and country code, area code and the number, without intervals. (Do not dial the 0 in front of area codes.)

— Some **area codes:** Britain 44; USA 1; Canada 1; Australia 61. To dial Britain: 9-9-44-Area Code-Number.

— Some **city codes:** İstanbul 1; Ankara 4; İzmir 51; Bodrum 6141; Marmaris 6121; Kuşadası 6361; Antalya 3111; Alanya 3231; Bursa 241; Van 061. To dial, say, Bursa: 9-241-number.

19 Clothing and Toiletries

a. Clothing **b.** Socks and Shoes **c.** Colours
d. Toiletries **e.** Hair Care

a.

elbise	*clothes, dress, costume*
kazak	*pullover, sweater*
etek	*skirt*
bulüz	*blouse*
gömlek	*shirt*
ti-şört	*T-shirt*
ceket	*jacket*
pantolon	*trousers*
şort	*shorts*
kemer	*belt*
kravat	*tie*
şapka	*hat*
atkı	*scarf (men)*
eldiven	*gloves*
eşarp	*scarf (women)*
yağmurluk	*raincoat*
palto	*coat*
mayo	*swimming suit/trunks*

Erkek/kadın elbisesi	*Men's/women's wear*
Bir gömlek almak istiyorum.	*I'd like a shirt.*
Ebadınız nedir?/Ölçünüz nedir?	*What is your size?*
Deneyebilirmiyim?	*Can I try it?*
Bu çok büyük/küçük/dar.	*It is too big/small/tight.*
Bu çok uzun/kısa.	*It's too long/short.*
Daha büyüğü/uzunu var mı?	*Is there a bigger/longer one?*
Bunun fiatı ne kadar?	*How much is this?*
Bu iyi./Bu iyi yakıştı.	*This is OK./That's smart.*
Bunu alıyorum.	*I'll take it.*
Kalsın, teşekkür ederim.	*I'll leave it, thank you.*

b. ayakkabı/kundura/pabuç | shoes
sandal | sandals
terlik | slippers
çorap (erkek/kadın çorabı) | socks/stockings (men's/ women's . . .)
külotlu çorap | tights

Bir (çift) ayakkabı/sandal almak istiyorum.	I'd like (a pair of) shoes/ sandals.
Kaç numara giyiyorsunuz?	What size do you take?
Bunun kahve rengisi var mı?	Do you do this in brown?

c. renk | colour
beyaz/siyah | white/black
gri/bej | grey/beige
kırmızı/yeşil | red/green
mavi/sarı | blue/yellow
kahve rengi/turuncu | brown/orange
d. sabun | soap
şampuan | shampoo
deterjan | detergent
havlu/deniz havlusu | towel/beach towel
diş macunu/diş fırçası | toothpaste/toothbrush
elektrikli traş makinası | electric shaver
jilet | razor blade
kolanya/limon kolanyası | cologne/lime cologne
kağıt mendil | paper tissues
hijyenik ped/kadın bağı | sanitary towel
tampon | tampon
prezervatif | condom
güneş yağı/kremi | sun tan oil/cream
gözlük/güneş gözlüğü | glasses/sun glasses
e. berber/kuaför | barber/women's hairdresser
saç/sakal/bıyık | hair/beard/moustache
tarak | comb
saç fırçası | hair brush

Saçımı kesermisiniz?	Can I have a hair cut?
Sakal traşı olmak istiyorum.	I'd like a shave.
Saçımı yaptırmak istiyorum.	I'd like to have my hair done.
Saçımı perma yaptırmak istiyorum.	I'd like to have my hair permed.

Money, Shopping→9

19 Clothing and Toiletries

1 What are these called in Turkish? Say you'd like to buy them.

2 Say the pullover is too short.

3 Ask if the assistant has anything bigger.

4 Say you'll take it.

5 How does the assistant ask what size you take?

What are the following called in Turkish? Ask the chemist
(**eczacı**) if she has them.
. . . var mı?

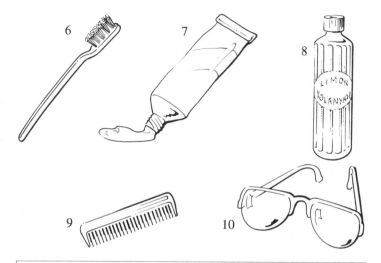

— When buying clothes and shoes, remember that Turkish sizes
are different from British ones.

Shoe sizes

British	1	2	3	4	5	6	7	8	9	10	11	12
Turkish	33	34–35	36	37	38	39–40	41	42	43	44	45	46

Dress sizes

British	10	12	14	16	18	20
Turkish	38	40	42	44	46	48

Collar sizes

British	13	$13\frac{1}{2}$	14	$14\frac{1}{2}$	15	$15\frac{1}{2}$	16	$16\frac{1}{2}$	17
Turkish	33	34	35–36	37	38	39	41	42	43

Suits, coats

British	36	38	40	42	44	46
Turkish	46	48	50	52	54	56

20 Accidents and Emergencies

a. Breakdowns, Accidents **b.** Theft **c.** Police
d. Doctor **e.** Illness **f.** Chemist **g.** Help

a. arıza	*breakdown*
garaj/araba tamircisi	*garage/car repairs; car mechanic*
kaza	*accident*
çarpışma	*collision*
sigorta	*insurance*

Arabam bozuldu.	*My car has broken down.*
Bir kaza oldu.	*There has been an accident.*
En yakın tamirhane/telefon nerede?	*Where is the nearest garage/telephone?*
Telefonu kullanabilirmiyim?	*Can I use the telephone?*
Polise haber verirmisiniz?	*Could you call the police?*
Şahitlik yaparmısınız?	*Would you be a witness?*

b. hırsızlık/soygun	*theft/robbery*
çalındı	*stolen*
kayboldu/kaybettim	*lost/I've lost*
unuttum	*I've forgotten*
cüzdan(ım)/para çanta(m)	*(my) wallet/(my) purse*

Anahtar(lar)ımı kaybettim.	*I've lost my key(s).*
Kayıp Eşya.	*Lost Property.*
Birisi paramı/çantamı çaldı.	*Somebody's stolen my money/bag.*

c. polis	*police(man)*
jandarma	*gendarmerie, rural military police*
karakol	*police station*
suç	*crime/offence*
avukat	*lawyer*

Polis çağırın!	*Call the police!*
Polis Bey/Memur Bey	*[addressing a policeman]*
Yardım edermisiniz?	*Can you help?*
Şikayetçiyim.	*I have a complaint.*

d. doktor/kadın doktor
 dişçi
 ambulans/cankurtaran
 hastane
 İlk Yardım
 Kızılay

doctor/lady doctor
dentist
ambulance
hospital
First Aid
Red Crescent [equivalent of
Red Cross]

Acele doktor çağırın!
Ciddi/Ciddi değil

Get a doctor, quick!
Serious/Not serious

---

e. hasta/hastalık
 güneş yanığı/güneş çarpması
 soğuk (almak)
 ishal/kabızlık
 kalp krizi

ill, sick/illness, sickness
sunburn/sunstroke
(to have a) cold
diarrhoea/constipation
heart attack

Rahatsızım./Hastayım.
Başım ağrıyor.
Midem ağrıyor.
Ateşim var.
Yaralandım./İncindim.
Ayağımı kestim.
Dişim ağrıyor.
Şuram ağrıyor.

I'm not well./I'm ill.
I have a headache.
I have a stomach-ache.
I have a fever.
I'm injured./I'm hurt.
I have cut my foot.
I have toothache.
I've got a pain here.

---

f. eczane
 ilaç/reçete
 merhem/krem
 hap/tablet
 uyku ilacı
 yara bandı

chemist/pharmacy
medicine/prescription
ointment/cream
tablet/pill
sleeping pill
bandage

Nöbetçi Eczane.
Bir yara bandı lütfen.

Chemist on emergency duty.
Some bandages, please.

---

g. Dikkat!/Tehlike!

Caution!/Danger!

İmdat!
Yangın var!
Yangın Çıkışı/Çıkış
Türkçe bilmiyorum!

Help!
Fire!
Fire Exit/Exit
I don't speak Turkish!

20 Accidents and Emergencies

1 You telephone a garage. Tell the mechanic that your car has broken down.

2 You are involved in an accident. How do you ask someone to call the police?

3 Ask where the nearest telephone is.

4 Tell the police you have lost your wallet.

5 Say that someone has stolen your camera.

6 You have witnessed an accident. How do you ask someone to call an ambulance?

7 You are not feeling well and go to the doctor. Tell him you have (a) a headache; (b) a cold; (c) cut your foot.

8 The doctor does not think it is serious. What does he say?

9 Ask the chemist for (a) some ointment; (b) a bottle of sleeping pills; (c) some bandages.

10 Tell the dentist you have toothache.

11 You are locked inside a building. What do you shout through the window?

12 The main exit is blocked. What sign do you look for?

— **Emergency telephone numbers:**
Emergency police telephone (in large cities): 055. Emergency gendarme (in small towns and rural areas): 081. Tourist Police and Security: There is a special police office in İstanbul to deal with tourists' problems. Tel: (1)528 5369.
— Emergency medical service: 077.
— Emergency fire service: 000.
Road rescue services (all along the Edirne–Ankara road, E-5): Edirne: (1811)1170, İstanbul: (1)353 3511, İzmit: (211)2330, Sakarya: (261)135 94, Ankara: (4)315 83 38. Additionally: Touring and Automobile Club: İstanbul: (1)146 7090, Ankara: (4)118 6578.

— **In case of accidents**, whether anyone is injured or not, a police report is required by Turkish insurance companies, so inform the police and ask for a report. There are many private garages even in small towns. Obtain a receipt if you want to claim your expenses.

— State **hospitals** deal with accidents and emergencies. They are either free or inexpensive. But, there is no reliable emergency ambulance service. In small towns the hospitals and other medical services may be rather basic. Private hospitals and all doctors and dentists charge for their services. There is no reciprocal health cover between Turkey and the UK, so take out adequate travel and/or health insurance before your departure. Obtain receipts for any payments. Chemists operate an emergency rota, and the names of local 'night chemists' (**Nöbetçi Eczane**) are displayed in the windows of all chemists.

— Some doctors, especially in university hospitals in large cities and those at seaside resorts, may speak some English, or know the language well enough to help you. Use the words and expressions introduced in sections **d**, **e** and **f** of this unit as well as the expressions below to communicate with them:

Doktor	*Doctor*	**Dişçi**	*Dentist*
Hastabakıcı	*Nurse*	**Eczane/Eczacı**	*Chemist*

Doktor bey/Doktor hanım	*Doctor (to male/female)*
Şuramı bir böcek ısırdı.	*An insect has bitten here.*
Burnum kanadı (kanıyor).	*My nose was (is) bleeding.*
Seyahate çıkabilirmiyim?	*Can I travel (i.e. in this condition)?*

baş(ım)	*(my) head*	**göz(ler)**	*eye(s)*
burun	*nose*	**kulak(lar)**	*ear(s)*
ağız	*mouth*	**boyun**	*neck*
mide(m)	*(my) stomach*	**kalb(im)**	*(my) heart*
boğaz	*throat*	**kol(lar)**	*arm(s)*
el(ler)	*hand(s)*	**parmak(lar)**	*finger(s)*
dirsek	*elbow*	**diz(ler)**	*knee(s)*
bacak(lar)	*arm(s)*	**ayak (ayaklar)**	*foot (feet)*
ayak parmağı	*toe*	**diş (dişler)**	*tooth (teeth)*
sağ/sol	*right/left*	**arka/ön**	*back/front*

Answers

1 General Expressions
1 Evet, benim (or, Evet hamfendi). 2 Hayır, ben değilim (or, Hayır beyefendi). 3 Evet, benim (or, Evet beyefendi).
4 Hayır, ben değilim (or, Hayır hamfendi). 5 İyi günler beyefendi. 6 İyi günler hamfendi. 7 Allaha ısmarladık.
8 Pasaportunuz lütfen. 9 Teşekkür ederim beyefendi.
10 Özür dilerim hamfendi. 11 Bu benim kocam George (Miller). 12 Bu benim eşim Val (Miller). 13 (a) Evet, teşekkür ederim. (b) Hayır, (şimdi içemem) teşekkür ederim.

2 Arriving in Turkey
1 valiz (or, bavul). 2 çanta. 3 Gümrüğe tâbi birşeyiniz var mı? 4 Hayır, yok. 5 Arabanızın arkasını açarmısınız?
6 Valizinizi açarmısınız? 7 Adım ... 8 Pasaportunuz lütfen? 9 Ehliyetiniz, lütfen. 10 Anlamadım. 11 Evet, İngilizim. 12 Tamam, buyrun. 13 Büyük Britanya (commonly, İngiltere). 14 Avustralya. 15 Türkiye.
16 İngiliz gazeteleri var mı?

3 Driving a Car
1 araba (or, otomobil). 2 kamyon. 3 Süper, Normal?
4 Doldurun, lütfen. 5 Yağ ve lastiklere bakarmısınız? 6 İyi yolculuklar. 7 Otoyol. 8 Hastane. 9 Park yeri.
10 Park Yapılmaz. 11 Benzin İstasyonu.

4 Finding Your Way
1 Kuzey, Güney, Doğu, Batı. 2 Bir İstanbul haritası lütfen.
3 Karayolları haritanız var mı acaba. 4 Karaköy yolu hangisi acaba? 5 Sağa dönün. 6 Sola dönün. 7 Doğru gidin.
8 Çok uzak mı? 9 DUR. 11 Sağ şerite geçerim.

5 Public Transport
1 DANIŞMA. 2 EMANET. 3 Gündüz otobüsü. 4 Otobüs durağı nerede?. 5 Antalya'ya bir bilet lütfen. 6 Boğaz Vapur İskelesi. 7 Yataklı vagon. 8 Havaalanı'na lütfen. 9 Dış Hatlar Terminali nerede? 10 Bir hamal lütfen. 11 Topkapı Sarayı'na kaça götürürsünüz? 12 Bilet gişesi nerede?

6 Accommodation
1 yatak. 2 anahtar. 3 İyi bir otel arıyorum. 4 Boş bir odanız var mı (acaba)? 5 Bir gecelik duşlu bir oda istiyorum.
6 Kahvaltı dahil ne kadar? 7. Çok pahalı. 8 fatura.
9 'G'. 10 Tuvaletler nerede? 11 Boş. 12 Meşgul.

7 Numbers, Weights and Measures
1 Onbeş. 2 Onyedi. 3 Yüzon. 4 İkiyüz oniki. 5 Beş

numaradan.　6　Sekiz numaradan.　7　İki numaradan.　8　Bir numaradan.　9　Üç numaradan.　10　(a) ikiyüz yirmidokuz kilometre,　(b) dörtyüz ellisekiz km.,　(c) ikiyüz kırkyedi km.,　(d) bin yetmişsekiz km.,　(e) dokuzyüz yetmişaltı km.,　(f) dokuzyüz otuziki km.　11　Bulgur Sokak, No Otuzdört, Daire Yedi, İstanbul.　12　Elmanın kilosu ne kadar?　13　Bir litrelik su istiyorum.　14　Yarım kilo domates lütfen.

8　Times and Dates
1　Saat kaç?　2　(a) Saat dokuz (or, Sabah saat dokuz), (b) Saat altı buçuk,　(c) Saat yediyi çeyrek geçiyor,　3　(a) Saat üç (or, Öğleden sonra saat üç),　(b) Saat dörde çeyrek var, (c) Saat yedi.　4　(a) Yirmi dakika,　(b) yarım saat,　(c) on gün, (d) altı ay.　5　Geceyarısı.　6　Uçak ne zaman hareket ediyor? 7　Pazartesi-Cuma saat dokuzdan beşe kadar; Cumartesi-Pazar saat ondan dörde kadar　8　Yirmibir Ağustos Bindokuzyüz seksen sekiz; Otuz Ekim Bindokuzyüz seksen sekiz.

9　Money and Shopping
1　KAMBİYO (also, EXCHANGE, WECHSEL).　2　Buyrun.　3　Bir havlu almak istiyorum.　4　Şu gömlek ne kadar?　5　Yirmi iki bin lira.　6　Başka arzunuz var mı?　7　Lütfen kasa'ya ödeyin.　8　Ne kadar ediyor?　9　(a) Yüz yedi lira,　(b) Üçbin kırkbeş lira.　10　(a) İkibin beşyüz doksansekiz lira, oniki kuruş; (b) İkibin altıyüz üç lira, otuz kuruş.

10　Meals
1　Kahvaltı, öğle yemeği, akşam yemeği.　2　(a) kahve fincanı, (b) çay bardağı,　(c) şişe,　(d) çatal,　(e) tabak,　(f) bıçak, (g) kaşık.　3　çay(lar).　4　Bir bardak beyaz şarap lütfen. 5　Biraz ekmek lütfen.　6　İki orta şekerli kahve lütfen.　7　Bir peynirli omlet lütfen.　8　İki dönerli sandviç lütfen.

11　Restaurants
1　(a) Pastacı, baklavacı veya tatlıcı　(b) Lokanta, restoran, kebapçı veya kafeterya,　(c) Bar, birahane veya meyhane.　2　Bir kişilik masanız var mı?　3　Yemek yemek istiyordum. 4　Yemek listesini rica edebilirmiyim (or, Yemek listesi lütfen). 5　Tuz lütfen.　6　Ne içersiniz?　7　Hesap lütfen.　8　Servis dahil mi?　9　Üstü kalsın.　10　(a) sandalye,　(b) masa. 11　Tuz, biber, kırmızı biber, kürdan.

12　Starters, Meat, Fish
1　Bir sebze çorbası lütfen.　2　Yalancı dolma lütfen.　3　Şiş kebap lütfen.　4　İyi pişmiş lütfen.　5　Yanında pilav lütfen.

Answers

6 Peynirli omlet lütfen. 7 Tavuklu pilav lütfen.
8 (a) pilav, (b) köfte. 9 GARDEN KEBAB – Ingredients: $\frac{1}{2}$ kg lamb cubed for skewering, 1 aubergine, 1 firm tomato, 2 green peppers, 1 onion, 2 spoonfuls of butter, black pepper, salt.

13 Vegetables, Fruit, Desserts

1 karpuz: Ben karpuzu severim. 2 üzüm: Ben üzümü severim. 3 elma: Ben elmayı severim. 4 portakal: Ben portakalı severim. 5 limon: Ben limonu severim. 6 patates: Ben patatesi severim. 7 havuç: Ben havucu severim.
8 domates: Ben domatesi severim. 9 patlıcan: Ben patlıcanı severim. 10 Biraz lokum almak istiyorum. 11 Bir baklava lütfen. 12 DONDURMACI. 13 Dondurmalı bir kazandibi lütfen. 14 baklava.

14 Drinking and Smoking

1 Kahve mi, çay mı istersiniz? 2 Orta şekerli iki kahve lütfen. 3 Bir paket sigara ve bir kibrit lütfen. 4 Biraz buz lütfen. 5 sigara. 6 kibrit. 7 çakmak. 8 kül tablası.
9 şişe. 10 şişe açacağı. 11 Bir ayran lütfen. 12 Bir şişe kırmızı şarap lütfen. 13 Bir soğuk bira lütfen. 14 Bir şişe maden suyu lütfen.

15 Sightseeing and Entertainment

1 Kaya mezarları (Rock tombs), Silifke. 2 Fairy chimneys, Ürgüp, Cappadocia. 3 İshakpaşa Sarayı. 4 Nemrut Dağı.
5 Turizm Danışma. 6 Tur ne zaman başlıyor? 7 Yedi'de başlıyor. 8 AÇILIŞ SAATLERİ. 9 GİŞE. 10 GİRİŞ.
11 ÇIKIŞ. 12 KAPALI.

16 Excursions and Recreation

1 Ayasofya'yı görüyorum. 2 Didim'deki Apollo tapınağını görüyorum. 3 Mevlana Türbesi'ni görüyorum. 4 (a) PLAJ, (b) YÜZME HAVUZU. 5 Bir şemsiye kiralamak istiyorum.
6 Bir şezlong kiralamak istiyorum. 7 Bir deniz yatağı kiralamak istiyorum. 8 Bir fotoğraf makinası almak istiyorum. 9 Bir filim almak istiyorum. 10 Bir filaş almak istiyorum.

17 Weather

1 güneşli. 2 Batı'da güneşli, Doğu'da bulutlu. 3 güneşli.
4 yağışlı. 5 güneşli.

18 Post Office and Telephone

1 kart-postal. 2 zarf. 3 adres. 4 pul. 5 posta kutusu. 6 jeton. 7 Avustralya için bir kart-postal pulu

Answers

lütfen. 8 Dörtyüz liralık üç pul lütfen. 9 Telefon numaranız kaç? 10 Alo, ben Gül. 11 telefon.
12 Orası . . . [number] . . . 'mı?; (or, for example: Orası Türk Hava Yolları mı? *Is that Turkish Airlines?*).

19 Clothing and Toiletries
1 (a) elbise: Bir elbise almak istiyorum. (b) kazak, (c) etek, (d) ceket, (e) pantolon, (f) gömlek (men), bulüz (women), (g) şapka, (h) mayo, (i) kemer. 2 Bu kazak çok kısa.
3 Bir büyüğü var mı? 4 Bunu alıyorum. 5 Kaç numara giyiyorsunuz? 6 Diş fırçası var mı? 7 Diş macunu var mı?
8 Kolanya var mı? 9 Tarak var mı? 10 Gözlük var mı?

20 Accidents and Emergencies
1 Alo, arabam bozuldu. 2 Bir kaza oldu. Polise haber verirmisiniz (or, Lütfen polis çağırın). 3 En yakın telefon nerede? 4 Cüzdanımı kaybettim. 5 Fotoğraf makinam çalındı. 6 Acele ambulans çağırın. 7 (a) Başım ağrıyor, (b) Soğuk almışım, (c) Ayağımı kesdim. 8 Ciddi değil.
9 (a) Bir merhem istiyorum, (b) Uyku habı istiyorum, (c) Yara bandı istiyorum. 10 Dişim ağrıyor. 11 İmdat! 12 YANGIN ÇIKIŞI (or, ÇIKIŞ).

Turkish–English Vocabulary

Note: Int. *refers to the numbered sections in the* Introduction to Turkish Grammar *at the beginning of the book.* Q *indicates questions, and* □ *indicates information boxes at the end of each unit.*

-a/-e to Int.7, 7b
ABD USA 2c
acele quick 20d
acı hot, spicy 10□
açık open 15d
açılış saatları opening hours 15d
ad name 1d, 1□, first name 2b
ada island 16b
adam man 1d
adres address 7
affedersiniz excuse me 1c
afiyet olsun bon appetit 10b
ağır araç (vasıta) heavy vehicles 3a
ağrı pain 20□
Ağustos August 8c
Akdeniz Mediterranean 16b
akşam evening 8a, 8b
akşam yemeği dinner, supper 10a
al(mak) take 19a
Allahaısmarladık goodbye 1b
alo (telf.) hello 18c
alçak basınç low-pressure area 17c
ambulans, cankurtaran ambulance 20d
Amerika(lı) America(n) 2c
Anadolu Anatolia 2c
anahtar key 1f, 6b, 20b
anla(mak) (to) understand 2c
anıt monument 15b
araba car Int.18, 19, 3a, etc.
araba sür(mek) (to) drive 3a
araba tamircisi garage 3d, 20a
arabanın bagajı boot 2a
arabanın evrakları car registration papers 2b
armut pear 13b
arıza breakdown 20a
asansör lift 6b
ateş fever 20e
atkı scarf 19a
avukat lawyer 20c

Avustralya(lı) Australia(n) 2c
ay month 8c
ayakkabı shoes 19b
az little 7b
az pişmiş rare (cooked) 12b

bagaj luggage 2a
bahçe park 16b
bahşiş tip 11d, 11□
bakkal grocer 9c, 9□
balık fish 12d
banka bank 9b
banliyö treni local trains 5a
banyo bathroom 6b
bardak glass 10b
başım headache
batı west 4d
Bay (WC, OO, tuvalet) gentlemen (WC) 6d
Bay Mr 1d
bay, bey gentleman 1d
Bayan (WC, OO, tuvalet) ladies (WC) 6d
Bayan Mrs/Ms 1d
bayan madam 1a, 1□, miss 1d
bayram religious or public festival 15□
bebek baby 1d
bedava free 1□, 9d
bekleme salonu waiting room 5a
bekçili garaj guarded car park 3d
belediye town hall 4b
ben I Int.4, 1f
benim my Int.5, 1f
benzin petrol 3c, 3□
berber barber, hairdresser 19e
beyaz white 19c
beyefendi sir 1a, 1□
bezelye peas 13a
bıçak knife 10b
biber pepper 11c

Turkish–English Vocabulary

biftek beefsteak 12b
bilet ticket 5a, 15d
bin thousand 7a
bır a, an Int.3, 1e
bir one 7a
bira beer 14b
birahane bar 11a
birşey anything 2a
biz we Int.4
Boğaziçi Bosphorus 15□, 16b
boş vacant 6d
bozdurmak cash (to) 9b
bozuk para small change 9a
börek pastry 13c
Britanya Britain 2c
broşür brochure 15a
bu this Int.6, 1e
bugün today 8b
bulut(lu) cloud(y) 17c
bulvar avenue, boulevard 4c
buyrun welcome, come in 1c, 9c
buz ice (drinks) 10□
büyük big 19a

cadde road 3b, 4c, street 4d
cankurtaran ambulance 20d
ceket jacket 19a
ceza fines 3□, 20□
ciddi serious 20d
Cuma Friday 8c
Cumartesi Saturday 18c
cüzdan purse 20b, wallet 9a

çakmak lighter 14c
çal(mak) (to) steal 20b
çarpışma collision 20a
Çarşamba Wednesday 8c
çatal fork 10b
çay tea 10c, 14a, 14□
çayhane tea house, cafe 11a
çek(iniz) pull 15d
çeyrek saat quarter of an hour 8a
çıkış exit 5d, 15d
çikolata chocolate 13c
çilek strawberry 10c, 13b
çips crisps 10d, 13a
çocuk(lar) child(ren) 1d

çok very much; —**teşekkür ederim**
  thank you very much 1c
çorba kasesi soup bowl 10b
çorba soup 12a

dağ mountain 16b
dağcılık mountain-climbing 16c
dakika minute 8a
damgalamak to stamp 18b
dana veal 12b
danışma enquiries, information 5e
dar tight 19a
-de/-da at, in on Int.9
deklare (to) declare 2a
demiryolları railways 5a
-den/-dan from Int.8
deniz sea 16b
derece degree 17b
dikkat caution 3b, 20g
dil balığı sole 12d
diş teeth 20e
dişçi dentist 20d
diş fırçası toothbrush 19d
diş macunu toothpaste 19d
dizel diesel 3c
doktor doctor 20d
dolmuş shared taxi 5d, 5□
dolu fully booked 6b
dolu hail 17d
domuz eti ham, pork 12b
don ice (weather) 17d
dondurma ice cream 13d
doğru gidiniz straight ahead 4d
doğu east 4d
dön(mek) (to) return Int.19,
  —**ticket** 5a
dön(üş) (to) turn 4d
döviz foreign currency 9b
duman, sigara dumanı smoke 3c,
  14c
dur stop 4c
duş shower 6b
dükkan shop 9c, 9□
dün yesterday 8b

eczane pharmacy 9□, 20f
eczane, eczacı chemist 20f
Ege (Denizi) Aegean (Sea) 16b

Turkish–English Vocabulary

ehliyet driving licence 2b, 2□
ekmek bread 10c
ekmekçi bakery 9□
ekspres tren express train 5a
el hand 20e
el çantası handbag 2a
elbise, entari dress, clothes 19a
eldiven gloves 19a
elektrikli traş makinası electric shaver 19d
elma apple 13b
elçilik embassy 2c
emanet(çi) left luggage 4a
emniyet kemeri seat belt 3□
enginar artichoke 13a
erkek man 1d
erkek çocuğu boy 1d
erkek çorabı socks 19b
eş wife/husband 1f
eşarp scarf 19a
et meat 12b
etek skirt 19a
ev house 4b
evet yes 1a, 2a

fatura bill 6c
festival festival 15c
fırça brush 19e
fırtına thunderstorm 17c
fiat price 6c, 9d
filim film 16d
filtre filter 14c
fincan cup 10b
filaş flash 16d
fotoğraf photo 16d, 16□
fotoğraf makinası camera 16d
Fransız French 2c

Galler/Galli Wales/Welsh 2c
gar station 5a
garson waiter 11d
gazete newspaper 2c
gece kulübü night club 15c
gece night 6b, 8b
geceyarısı midnight 8b
gecikme delay 5e
gemi boat, ship 5c, 16c
gençlik yurdu youth hostel 6a

getir(mek) (to) bring 11d
gezi excursion, outing 16a; sightseeing tour 4b
gidebilirsiniz go on 2a
giriş entrance 15d
giriş katı, birinci kat ground floor 6b
gişe cashier (ticket office) 5a, 15d; counter 18a
git(mek) (to) go Int.18,19, 3a, etc.
giyecek clothes 19a
gri grey 19c
göl lake 16c
gölge shade 17b
gömlek shirt 9a, 19a
gönderen sender 18b
görülecek yer(ler) sights 15b
gözlük glasses 19d
gümrük customs 2a
gün day 8b
günaydın good morning 1b
güney south 4d
güneş sun 17b
güneş çarpması sunstroke 20e
güneş yanığı sunburn 20e
güneş yağı/kremi suntan oil/cream 19d
güneşte yan(mak) (to) tan 16c
güverte deck 5c
güzel beautiful, good 17b

haber ver(mek) (to) report 20a
hamal porter 5a
hamfendi madam 1a, 1□
hamur tatlısı (sweet) pastry 13c
hangi which Int.15
hap tablet 20f
harita map 4a
hasta ill, sick 20e
hastane hospital 20c
haşlama stew 12b
hava weather 17a,b,c
hava açılıyor clearing up 17c
hava tahmini weather forecast 17a
havaalanı, hava limanı airport 5b
havlu towel 19d
hayır no Int.14, 1a, 2a
hergün every day 8b

Turkish–English Vocabulary

hesap bill 11d
hırsızlık theft 20b
hijyenik ped/kadın bağı sanitary towel 19d
hoşgeldiniz welcome 1b
hoşçakalın goodbye 1b
hüviyet identity 1b

ırmak river 16b
içecek refreshments, beverages 14a
için for Int.7, 6b, 18b
içinde in Int.9
içki drink 10a, 14a, 14b
içki listesi wine list 11b
ikindi çayı afternoon tea 10a
ilaç medicine 20f
-ile with Int.18, 1□, 6b, 14c
İLK YARDIM Emergency, First Aid 20d, 20□
İMDAT! Help! 20g
-in/-nin of Int.10
incindi hurt 20e
İngiliz English, British (person or thing) 1c
İngiltere England 1c
ishal diarrhoea 20e
isim (first) name 1d, 1□, 2b
İskoç(ya) Scottish, Scotland 2c
istasyon station 5a
istiridye oysters 12d
it(iniz) push 15d
iyi akşamlar good evening 1b
iyi geceler good night 1b
iyi well 1b, 2a; good 6a
iyi günler good afternoon/good day/hello 1b
iyi pişmiş well-done (cooked) 12b

jeton telephone token 18c
jetonlu telefon telephone box 18c

kabızlık constipation 20e
kabin cabin 5c
kaç tane how many Int.15, 7b, 1a
kaça/ne kadar how much Int.15, 3c, 6c, 9d
kadın woman 1d
kadın çorabı stockings 19b

kağıt mendil tissues 19d
kahvaltı breakfast 6c, 10a, 10□
kahve coffee (Turkish) 10b,c, 14a, 14□
kahve(hane)/çayhane café, tea shop 11a
kakao cocoa 10c
kale castle 15b
kalkış departure 5e
kalp krizi heart attack 20e
kamara cabin 5c
kambiyo currency exchange 9b
kamp yeri camp site 6a, 6□
kamyon lorry 3a
kapalı closed 8c, 15d; overcast 17c
kar snow 17d
Karadeniz Black Sea 16b
karakol police station 20c
karavan caravan 3a
karı(-m/-sı) (my/his) wife 1f
karides shrimps 12d
kart-postal postcard 18b
kasa cash register, cashier 9d
kasap butcher 9□
kase bowl 10b
kaşık spoon 10b
kat floor, storey 6b
kavun melon 13b
kaya(lık) rock 16b
kaybet(mek) (to) lose 20b
kaza accident 20a, 20□
kaza servisi rescue service 3□, 20□
kazak sweater 19a
kebap kebab 12b
kemer belt 19a
kent town 4b
kesik, kesilmek (to) cut 20e
Kıbrıs Cyprus 2c
kırmızı red 19c
kısa short 19a
kız girl 1d
kızarmış patates chips 10d, 13a
kibrit match 14c
kilise church 15b
kilometre kilometre 7b, 7
kim(in) who(se) Int.15
kimlik identity 1b

Turkish–English Vocabulary

kirala(mak) (to) hire 16c
kiralık araba car rental 3a
koca husband 1f
kolanya eau de cologne 19d
konsolosluk consulate 2c
koru(luk) wood 16b
koyun/kuzu eti lamb 12b
köprü bridge 4c
kötü bad 17c
köy village 4b
kredi kartı credit card 9b
krema cream 13c
kuaför hairdresser 19e
kule tower 15b
kundura shoes 19b
kuşetli vagon couchettes car 5a
kutu box 14c
kuzey north 4d
küçük little 7b; small 19a
küçük şişe half-bottle 14b
kül tablası ashtray 14c
külotlu çorap tights 19b

lahana cabbage 13a
lastik(ler) tyre(s) 3c
liman port 5c
limon lemon 10c, 13b, 14a
lokum Turkish Delight 13c, 13Q
lütfen please 1c

madeni para coin 9a
mağara cave 16b
mağaza (büyük) department store
  9c
mantar mushroom 13a
market supermarket 9c
Marmara (Denizi) Marmara (Sea)
  16b
marmelat marmalade 10c
marul, salata lettuce 13a
masa table 11a
masa örtüsü tablecloth 10b
mavi blue 19c
mayo swimming costume 19a
mecburi istikamet diversion 3b
mektup letter 18b
memnun oldum pleased to . . . 1☐
mendil handkerchief 19d

merdiven stairs 16b
merhaba hello 1b
merhem ointment 20f
meydan square
meyva fruit 10c, 13b
meyva suyu juice 10c, 14a
meze appetizer 11b
meşgul engaged (toilet) 6d
meşrubat beverages 14a
midem stomach ache 20e
midye mussels 12d
milliyet nationality 2c
mimarlık architecture 15b
morina cod 12c
motel motel 6a
muz banana 13b
müze museum 15b, 12☐

nasıl how Int.15, 1b
ne what Int.15, etc.
nehir river 16b
nerede where Int.15, 4c, 4d, etc.
neskafe coffee (instant) 14a
ne zaman when Int. 15, 8b
niçin, neden why Int. 15
numara size 19b

oda room 6b
oda ayırt(mak) (to) reserve a room
  6b
oda numarası room number 6b
omlet omelette 10d
on ten 7a
onlar they Int.4
'OO' (yüz numara) toilets 6d
orman forest 16b
orta pişmiş medium (cooked) 12b
Osmanlı Ottoman 15b
otel hotel 6a
otobüs bus 5d
otobüs durağı bus stop 5d
otogar bus terminal 5d, 5☐
otomobil car Int.18, 19, 3a, etc.
otoyol motorway 3b
oturduğunuz yer place of residence
  2b

öde(mek) (to) pay 6c, 9d

Turkish–English Vocabulary

öğle noon 8b
öğle yemeği lunch 10a
öğleden sonra afternoon 8a, 8b
öğün meal 10a
ölçü size 19a

pahalı expensive 6c, 9d
palto coat 19a
pamuk cotton wool 19d
pansiyon guest house 6a
pantolon trousers 19a
para money 9a
para değiştir(mek) (to) change
  foreign currency 9b
park park 16b
park etmek to park 3d, 3□
park yapılmaz no parking 3d
park yeri parking 3d, 3□
pasaport passport 2b
pasta cake 13c
pastacı, pastahane cake shop 9□,
  11□
patates potatoes 13a
Pazar Sunday 8c
pazar market 9c, 9
Pazartesi Monday 8c
peçete napkin 10b
peron platform 5a
Perşembe Thursday 8c
peynir cheese 10d, 11b
pil battery 16d
pirinç pilavı rice pilav 13a
plaj beach 16c
polis police(man) 20c
portakal orange 13b
portakal suyu orange juice 14a
postahane (PTT) post office 18a
posta kutusu letter box 18a
prezervatif condom 19d
pul stamp 18b
pulman pullman 5a

reçel jam, marmalade 10c
reçete prescription 20f
rehber guide 15d
renk colour 19c
resepsiyon reception desk 6b
rosto roast meat 12□

rötar delay 5e
rüzgar wind 17c

saat clock, watch, hour 8a, 8□
sabah(leyin) morning 8a, 8b
saç traşı haircut 19e
sağ right 4d
sağanak shower 17c
sağol(un) thank you 1c
sahil coast 16b
salçalı gravy 12b
Salı Tuesday 8c
sanat art 15b
sandalye chair 11a
sandviç/tost sandwich 10d
saray palace 15b
sarı yellow 19c
sarımsak garlic 13a
satın al(mak) (to) buy 9c
sebze(ler) vegetables 13a
self-servis self-service 9c
serbest (taksi) free (taxi) 5d
sergi exhibition 15b
servis course 11b; service 11d
seyahat acentası travel agency 15a
seyahat çeki travellers cheque 9b
sıcak hot (warm) 17b
sığır eti beef 12b
-sız without Int.18, 1□, 14c
sigara cigarettes 14c
sigara iç(mek) (to) smoke 14c
sigara içilmez no smoking 3c, 14c
sigorta insurance 20a
sinema cinema 15c
sinema filmi cine film 16d
sis fog 17c
siyah black 19c
siz (sen) you Int.14, 1f
sizin(ki) your(s) Int.5, 1f
sol left 4d
sosis sausage 10d
soğan onion 12a, 13a
soğuk cold (illness) 17d; **soğuk
  al(mak)** (to) have a cold 20e
stadyum stadium 15c
sterlin pound sterling 9b
su water 10b, 14□, 17b
su kayağı water skiing 16c

Turkish–English Vocabulary

sucuk Turkish-style sausage 10d
suç offence 20c
sürahi jug 10b
sürat tahdidi speed limit 3□
süt milk 7b, 10c, 14a

şampanya champagne 14b
şampuan shampoo 19d
şapka hat 19a
şarap wine 10b, 14b
şehir town 4b
şehir haritası street map 4a
şehirlerarası tren long-distance train 5a
şehir merkezi, centrum city centre 4b
şeker sugar 11c, 13b
şemsiye umbrella 17c
şerit track 5a
şikayet complaint 20c
şişe bottle 10b, 14b
şişe açacağı bottle opener 14b
şort shorts 19a
şu that Int.6, 1e

tabak dish, plate 10b
tabiiyet nationality 2c
taksi taxi 5d, 5□
tam pansiyon full board 6c
tampon tampon 19d
tarak comb 19e
tarife timetable 5e
tatlı dessert 11b
tatlı, şekerleme sweet 13c
tavuk chicken 12c
taşıyıcı porter 5d
TC (Türkiye Cumhuriyeti) Turkish Republic 2c
tehlike danger 3b, 20g
tek yön one-way street 4c
telefon numarası telephone number 18c
telefon rehberi telephone directory 18c
Temmuz July 8c
teras terrace 11a
tereyağı butter 7c, 10c

teşekkür ederim thank you 1b, 1c, 9c
tirbişon bottle opener 14b
tiyatro theatre 15c
tost toasted sandwich 10d
trafik traffic 3a, 3□
trafik işaretleri road signs 4c, 4d, 4□
trafik ışıkları traffic lights 4c
tren train 5a
Turizm Danışma tourist information office 15a
tuvalet toilets 6d
tuvalet kağıdı toilet roll, tissue 6d
tuz salt 11c
Türk/Türkiyeli Turk/Turkish 2c
Türkçe Turkish (lang.) Int.13, 2c, 20g
Türkiye Turkey 2c

ucuz cheap 9d
uçak aeroplane 5b
uçak yolculuğu air travel 5b
uçuş flight 5b
unut(mak) (to) forget 20b
uskumru mackerel 12d
uyku ilacı sleeping pill 20f
uyruk nationality 2c
uzak far 4d
uzun long 19a

ücretli yol toll road 3b
üstünde on Int.9
üzüm grape 13b

vagon coach 5d
valiz suitcase 1e, 1f
vapur ship 5c
var (to) have, there is Int.17
varış arrival 5e
ve and Int. 19
veya or Int.5
video (bandı) video (tape) 16d
vilayet town hall 4b
viraj bend 4d
vişne cherry 10c, 13b
voltaj electric voltage 6□

Turkish–English Vocabulary

yağ oil 3c, 11c
yağmur rain 17c
yağmurluk raincoat 19a
yakın near 4d
yakışıklı, yakıştı smart 19a
yangın fire 20g
yangın çıkışı emergency (fire) exit 15d
yara bandı bandage, plaster 20f
yaralı injured 20e
yarım half 8a
yarım pansiyon half-board 6c
yarım saat half an hour 8a
yarın tomorrow 8b
yatak bed 6b
yataklı vagon sleeping car 5a
yavaş slow down 3b
yelkenli sailing boat 16c
ye(mek) (to) eat a meal 10a, 11a
yemek ısmarla(mak) (to) order food 11b
yemek listesi menu 11b

yemek salonu dining room 10a
yemekli vagon dining car 5a
yeşil green 19c
yeşil fasulye runner beans 13a
yıl year 8c
yiyecek food 9
yol road 3b, 4c
yol hakkı right-of-way 3b
yol tamiratı road works 3b
yön direction 4d
yumurta egg 12c
yüksek basınç high pressure area 17b
yürü(mek) (to) walk 16c
yürüyüş(e çıkmak) (to) stroll 16c
yüz hundred 7a
yüz(mek) (to) swim 16c
yüzme havuzu swimming pool 16c

zaman time 8
zemin katı ground floor 6b
ziyaret (etmek) (to) visit 15d

English–Turkish Vocabulary

Note: Int. *refers to the numbered sections in the* Introduction to Turkish Grammar *at the beginning of the book.* Q *indicates questions, and* □ *indicates information boxes at the end of each unit.*

a, an bir Int.3, 1e
accident kaza 20a, 20□
address adres 7
Aegean (Sea) Ege (Denizi) 16b
aeroplane uçak 5b
afternoon öğleden sonra 8a,b
air travel uçak yolculuğu 5b
airport havaalanı, hava limanı 5b
ambulance ambulans, cankurtaran 20d
America(n) Amerika(lı) 2c
Anatolia Anadolu 2c
and ve Int.19
anything birşey 2a
appetiser meze 11b
apple elma 13b
architecture mimarlık 15b
arrival varış 5e
art sanat 15b
artichoke enginar 13a
ashtray kül tablası 14c
at -de/-da Int.9
August Ağustos 8c
Australia(n) Avustralya(lı) 2c
avenue bulvar 4c

baby bebek 1d
bad kötü 17c
bakery ekmekçi 9□
banana muz 13b
bandage yara bandı 20f
bank banka 9b
bar bar, meyhane, birahane 11a
barber berber, kuaför 19e
bathroom banyo 6b
battery pil 16d
beach plaj 16c
bed yatak 6b
beef sığır eti 12b
beefsteak biftek 12b
beer bira 14b
belt kemer 19a
bend viraj 4d

beverages meşrubat, içecek 14a
big büyük, geniş 19a
bill hesap 11d; fatura 6c
black siyah 19c
Black Sea Karadeniz 16b
blue mavi 19c
boat gemi 5c, 16c
boot arabanın bagajı 2a
Bosphorus Boğaziçi 15□, 16b
bottle şişe 10b, 14b
bottle opener şişe açacağı, tirbişon 14b
boulevard bulvar 4c
bowl kase 10b
box kutu 14c
boy erkek çocuğu 1d
bread ekmek 10c
breakdown arıza 20a
breakfast kahvaltı 6c, 10a, 10□
bridge köprü 4c
bring (to) getir(mek) 11d
British, Britain İngiliz, Britanya 2c
brochure broşür 15a
brush fırça 19e
bus otobüs 5d
bus stop otobüs durağı 5d
bus terminal otogar 5d, 5□
butcher kasap 9□
butter tereyağı 7c, 10c
buy (to) satın al(mak) 9c

cabbage lahana 13a
cabin kabin, kamara 5c
cafe kahvehane, çayhane 11a
cake pasta 13c
cake shop pastacı, pastahane 9
camera fotoğraf makinası 16d
camp site kamp yeri 6a, 6□
can/cannot (see Int.16)
car araba, otomobil Int.18, 19, 3a, etc.
caravan karavan 3a

English–Turkish Vocabulary

car registration papers arabanın
   evrakları 2b
car rental kiralık araba 3a
cash (to) bozdur(mak) 9b
cashier kasa 9d
cashier (ticket office) gişe 15d
cash register, cashier kasa 9d
castle kale 15b
caution dikkat 3b, 20g
cave mağara 16b
chair sandalye 11a
champagne şampanya 14b
cheap ucuz 9d
cheese peynir 10d, 11b
chemist eczane, eczacı 9□, 20f
cherry vişne 10c, 13b
chicken tavuk 12c
child(ren) çocuk(lar) 1d
chips kızarmış patates 10d, 13a
chocolate çikolata 13c
church kilise 15b
cine film sinema filmi 16d
cinema sinema 15c
city centre şehir merkezi, centrum
   4b
clearing up (weather) hava açılıyor
   17c
clock saat 8a, 8□
closed kapalı 8c, 15d
clothes giyecek, elbise 19a
cloud(y) bulut(lu) 17c
coach vagon 5d
coast sahil 16b
coat palto 19a
cocoa kakao 10c
cod morina 12c
coffee (Turkish) kahve 10b,c, 14a,
   14□
coffee (instant) neskafe 14a
coin madeni para 9a
cold (illness) soğuk 17d; **(to) have a
   cold** soğuk al(mak) 20e
collision çarpışma 20a
cologne (eau de) kolanya 19d
colour renk 19c
comb tarak 19e
complaint şikayet 20c
condom prezervatif 19d

constipation kabızlık 20e
consulate konsolosluk 2c
couchettes car kuşetli vagon 5a
counter gişe 18a
course servis 11b
cream krema 13c
credit card kredi kartı 9b
crisps çips 10d, 13a
cup fincan 10b
currency exchange kambiyo 9b
customs gümrük 2a
cut kesik, kesilmek 20e
Cyprus Kıbrıs 2c

danger tehlike 3b, 20g
day gün 8b
deck güverte 5c
declare (to) deklare (etmek) 2a
degree derece 17b
delay gecikme, rötar 5e
dentist dişçi 20d
department store büyük mağaza 9c
departure kalkış 5e
dessert tatlı 11b
diarrhoea ishal 20e
diesel dizel 3c
dining car yemekli vagon 5a
dining room yemek salonu 10a
dinner akşam yemeği 10a
direction yön, istikamet 4d
dish tabak 10b
diversion mecburi istikamet 3b
doctor doktor 20d
dress elbise, entari 19a
drink içki 10a, 14a, 14b
drinks (beverages) meşrubat, içecek
   10a, 14a
drive (to) araba sür(mek) 3a
driving licence ehliyet 2b, 2□

east doğu 4d
eat (to) ye(mek) 10a, 11a
egg yumurta 12c
electric voltage voltaj 6□
electric shaver elektrikli traş
   makinası 19d
embassy elçilik 2c
emergency ilk yardım 20d, 20□

English–Turkish Vocabulary

emergency (fire) exit yangın çıkışı
  20d
engaged (toilet) meşgul 6d
England İngiltere 1c
English person İngiliz 1c
enquiries danışma 5e
entrance giriş 15d
evening akşam 8a, 8b
every day hergün 8b
exchange kambiyo 9b
excursion gezi 16a
excuse me affedersiniz 1c
exhibition sergi 15b
exit çıkış 5d, 15d
expensive pahalı 1, 6c, 9d
express train ekspres tren 5a

far uzak 4d
festival festival 15c; bayram 15☐
fever ateş 20e
film filim 16d
filter filtre 14c
fines ceza 3☐
fire yangın 20g
first aid ilk yardım 20d
first name ad, isim 2b
fish balık 12d
flash filaş 16d
flight uçuş 5b
floor kat 6b
fog sis 17c
food yiyecek 9
for için Int.7, 6b, 18b
foreign currency döviz 9b
forest orman 16b
forget (to) unut(mak) 20b
fork çatal 10b
free bedava 1☐, 9d
free (taxi) serbest 5d
French Fransız 2c
Friday Cuma 8c
from -den/-dan Int.8
full board tam pansiyon 6c
fruit meyva 10c, 13b
fully booked dolu 6b

garage araba tamircisi 3d, 20a
garlic sarımsak 13a

gentleman bay, bey 1d
gentlemen (WC) Bay (WC, OO,
  tuvalet) 6d
girl kız 1d
glass bardak 10b
glasses gözlük 19d
gloves eldiven 19a
go (to) git(mek) Int.18, 19, 3a, etc.
good iyi 6a; güzel 17b
good afternoon iyi günler 1b
goodbye hoşçakalın,
  Allahaısmarladık 1b
good day iyi günler 1b
good evening iyi akşamlar 1b
good morning günaydın 1b
good night iyi geceler 1b
go on gidebilirsiniz 2a
grape üzüm 13b
gravy salçalı 12b
green yeşil 19c
grey gri 19c
grocer's bakkal 9c, 9☐
ground floor giriş katı, birinci kat
  6b
guarded car park bekçili garaj 3d
guest house pansiyon 6a
guide rehber 15d

hail dolu 17d
hairdresser kuaför, berber 19e
half yarım 8a
half an hour yarım saat 8a
half board yarım pansiyon 6c
half-bottle küçük şişe 14b
ham domuz eti 12b
hand el 20☐
handbag el çantası 2a
handkerchief mendil 19d
hat şapka 19a
have (to) var Int.17
headache baş ağrısı 20e
heart attack kalp krizi 20e
heavy vehicles ağır araç (vasıta) 3a
hello merhaba, iyi günler 1b, alo
  18c
help imdat 20g
high-pressure area yüksek basınç
  17b

English–Turkish Vocabulary

hire (to) kirala(mak) 16c
hospital hastane 20c
hot (warm) sıcak 17b; **(spicy)** acı 10□
hotel otel 6a
hour saat 8a
house ev 4b
how nasıl Int.15, 1b
how many kaç tane Int.15, 7b, 1a
how much ne kadar Int.15, 3c, 6c, 9d
hundred yüz 7a
hurt incindi 20e
husband eş, koca 1f

I ben Int.4, 1f
ice (weather) don, buz 17d; **(drinks)** buz 10□
ice cream dondurma 13d
ill hasta 20e
in içinde, -de/-da Int.9
information (enquiries) danışma 5e
injured yaralı 20e
insurance sigorta 20a
island ada 16b

jacket ceket 19a
jam reçel 10c
jug sürahi 10b
juice meyva suyu 10c, 14a
July Temmuz 8c

kebab kebap 12b
key anahtar 1f, 6b, 20b
kilometer kilometre 7b
knife bıçak 10b

ladies (WC) Bayan (WC, OO, tuvalet) 6d
lake göl 16c
lamb koyun, kuzu eti 12b
lawyer avukat 20c
left sol 4d
left luggage emanet(çi) 4a
lemon limon 10c, 13b, 14a
letter mektup 18b
letterbox posta kutusu 18a
lettuce marul, salata 13a

lift asansör 6b
lighter çakmak 14c
little az, küçük 7b
local trains banliyö treni 5a
long uzun 19a
long-distance train şehirlerarası treni 5a
lorry kamyon 3a
lose (to) kaybet(mek) 20b
low-pressure area alçak basınç 17c
luggage bagaj 2a
lunch öğle yemeği 10a

mackerel uskumru 12d
madam bayan, hamfendi 1a, 1□
man adam, erkek 1d
map harita 4a
market market, pazar 9c
marmalade marmelat, reçel 10c
Marmara (Sea) Marmara (Denizi) 16b
match kibrit 14c
meal yemek, öğün 10a
meat et 12b
medicine ilaç 20f
Mediterranean Akdeniz 16b
medium (cooked) orta pişmiş 12b
melon kavun 13b
men (WC) Bay 6d
menu yemek listesi 11b
midnight geceyarısı 8b
milk süt 7b, 10c, 14a
minute dakika 8a
miss bayan 1d
Monday Pazartesi 8c
money para 9a
month ay 8c
monument anıt 15b
morning sabah(leyin) 8a, 8b
motorway otoyol 3b
motel motel 6a
mountain dağ 16b
mountain-climbing dağcılık 16c
Mr Bay 1d
Mrs/Ms Bayan 1d
museum müze 12□, 15b
mushroom mantar 13a
mussels midye 12d

English–Turkish Vocabulary

my benim Int.5, 1f

name isim, ad 1d, 1□, 2b
napkin peçete 10b
nationality tabiiyet, uyruk, milliyet 2c
near yakın 4d
newspaper gazete 2c
night gece 6b, 8b
night club gece kulübü 15c
no hayır Int.14, 1a, 2a
no parking park yapılmaz 3d
no smoking sigara içilmez 3c, 14c
noon öğle 8b
north kuzey 4d

of -in/-nin Int.10
offence suç 20c
oil yağ 3c, 11c
ointment merhem 20f
omelette omlet 10d
on üstünde, -de/-da Int.9
one bir 7a
one-way street tek yön 4c
onion soğan 12a, 13a
open açık 15d
opening hours açılış saatleri 15d
or veya Int.5
orange portakal 13b
orange juice portakal suyu 14a
order (food) yemeği ısmarlamak 11b
Ottoman Osmanlı 15b
outing gezi, gezinti 16a
overcast kapalı 17c
oysters istiridye 12d

packet of cigarettes (bir) paket sigara 14c
pain ağrı 20□
pair of shoes (bir) çift ayakkabı 19b
palace saray 15b
park park, bahçe 16b
parking park yeri, park etmek 3d, 3□
passport pasaport 2b, 20b
pastry börek, (sweet) hamur tatlısı 13c

pay (to) öde(mek) 6c, 9d
pear armut 13b
peas bezelye 13a
pepper biber 11c
petrol benzin 3c, 3□
pharmacy eczane 20f
photo fotoğraf 16d, 16□
place of residence oturduğunuz yer 2b
plaster yara bandı 20f
plate tabak 10b
platform peron 5a
please lütfen 1c
pleased to . . . memnun oldum 1□
police(man) polis 20c
police station karakol 20c
pork domuz eti 12b
port liman 5c
porter hamal, taşıyıcı 5a
postcard kart-postal 18b
post office postahane (PTT) 18a
potatoes patates 13a
pound (£) sterlin 9b
prescription reçete 20f
price fiat 6c, 9d
pull çek(iniz) 15d
pullman pulman 5a
purse cüzdan 20b
push it(iniz) 15d

quarter of an hour çeyrek saat/onbeş dakika 8a
quick acele 20d

railways demiryolları 5a
rain yağmur 17c
raincoat yağmurluk 19a
rare (cooked) az pişmiş 12b
reception desk resepsiyon 6b
red kırmızı 19c
refreshments, beverages meşrubat, içecek 14a
report (to) haber ver(mek) 20a
rescue service kaza servisi 3□, 20□
return (to) dön(mek) Int.19,
   —**ticket** 5a
rice pirinç, pilav 13a

English–Turkish Vocabulary

right sağ 4d
right-of-way yol hakkı 3b
river nehir, ırmak 16b
road yol, cadde, sokak 3b, 4c
road signs trafik işaretleri 4c
road works yol tamiratı 3b
roast meat rosto 12□
rock kaya(lık) 16b
room oda 6b
room number oda numarası 6b
runner beans yeşil fasulye 13a

sailing boat yelkenli 16c
salt tuz 11c
sandwich sandviç, tost 10d
sanitary towel hijyenik ped/kadın bağı 19d
Saturday Cumartesi 18c
sausage sosis, sucuk 10d
scarf atkı, eşarp 19a
Scottish, Scotland İskoç(ya) 2c
sea deniz 16b
seat belt emniyet kemeri 3□
self-service self-servis 9c
sender gönderen 18b
serious ciddi 20d
service servis 11d
service station benzin (servis) istasyonu 3c
shade gölge 17b
shampoo şampuan 19d
ship gemi, vapur 5c
shirt gömlek 9a, 19a
shoes ayakkabı, kundura 19b
shop dükkan 9c, 9□
short kısa 19a
shorts şort 19a
shower duş 6b; sağanak 17c
shrimps karides 12d
sick hasta 20e
sights görülecek yer(ler) 15b
sightseeing tour gezi, tur 4b
sir beyefendi 1a, 1□
size ölçü 19a; numara 19b
skirt etek 19a
sleeping car yataklı vagon 5a
sleeping pill uyku ilacı 20f
slow down yavaş 3b

small change bozuk para 9a
smart yakışıklı, yakıştı 19a
smoke duman, sigara dumanı 3c, 14c
smoke (to) sigara iç(mek) 14c
snow kar 17d
socks erkek çorabı 19b
sole dil balığı 12d
soup çorba 12a
soup bowl çorba kasesi 10b
south güney 4d
speed limit sürat tahdidi 3□
spoon kaşık 10b
square meydan 4c
stadium stadyum 15c
stairs merdiven 6b
stamp pul; **to stamp** damgalamak 18b
station istasyon, gar 5a
steal (to) çal(mak) 20b
stew haşlama 12b
stockings kadın çorabı 19b
stop dur 4c
storey kat 6b
straight ahead doğru gidiniz 4d
strawberry çilek 10c, 13b
street cadde 4c, 4d
street map şehir haritası 4a
stroll yürüyüş(e çıkmak) 16c
sugar şeker 11c, 13b
suitcase valiz 1e, 1f
sun güneş 17b
sunburn güneş yanığı 20e
Sunday Pazar 8c
sunstroke güneş çarpması 20e
suntan oil/cream güneş yağı/kremi 19d
supermarket market, bakkal 9c
supper akşam yemeği 10a
sweater kazak 19a
sweet tatlı, şekerleme 13c
swim yüz(mek) 16c
swimming costume mayo 19a
swimming pool yüzme havuzu 16c

table masa 11a
tablecloth masa örtüsü 10b
tablet tablet, hap 20f

English–Turkish Vocabulary

take (to) al(mak) 19a
tampon tampon 19d
tan (to) güneşte yan(mak) 16c
taxi taksi, dolmuş 5d, 5☐
tea çay 10c, 14a, 14☐
tea (afternoon) ikindi çayı 10a
tea shop çayhane, kahve(hane) 11a
teeth diş 20e
telephone box telefon kulübesi 18c
telephone directory telefon rehberi 18c
telephone number telefon numarası 18c
telephone token jeton 18c
ten on 7a
terrace teras 11a
thank you teşekkür ederim 1b, 1c, 9c; sağol(un) 1c
theatre tiyatro 15c
they onlar Int.4
this, that bu, şu Int.6, 1e
thousand bin 7a
thunderstorm fırtına 17c
Thursday Perşembe 8c
ticket bilet 5a, 15d
ticket office/window bilet gişesi, gişe 5a, 15d
tight küçük, dar 19a
tights külotlu çorap 19b
time (telling-) saat, zaman 8
timetable tarife 5e
tip bahşiş 11d, 11☐
tissues kağıt mendil 19d
to -den, -dan Int.7, 7b
toasted sandwich tost 10d
today bugün 8b
toilet roll, tissue tuvalet kağıdı 6d
toilets tuvalet, 'OO' 6d
toll road ücretli yol 3b
tomorrow yarın 8b
toothbrush diş fırçası 19d
toothpaste diş macunu 19d
tour/excursion tur, gezi, ziyaret 15d
tourist information office Turizm Danışma 15a
towel havlu 19d
tower kule 15b
town şehir, kent 4b

town hall belediye, vilayet 4b
track şerit 5a
traffic trafik 3a, 3☐
traffic lights trafik ışıkları 4c
traffic police trafik polisi 3☐
train tren 5a
travel agency seyahat acentası 15a
travellers cheque seyahat çeki 9b
trousers pantolon 19a
truck kamyon 3a
Tuesday Salı 8c
turn dön(üş) 4d
Turkish Republic Türkiye Cumhuriyeti (TC) 2c
Turkey Türkiye 2c
Turk/Turkish Türk/Türkiyeli 2c
Turkish coffee kahve 10b,c, 14a, 14☐
Turkish Delight lokum 13c, 13Q10
Turkish (lang.) Türkçe Int.13, 2c, 20g
tyres lastik(ler) 3c

umbrella şemsiye 17c
understand (to) anla(mak) 2c
USA ABD 2c

vacant boş 6d
veal dana 12b
vegetables sebze(ler) 13a
very much çok; (thank you—) teşekkür ederim 1c
video (tape) video (bandı) 16d
village köy 4b
visit (to) ziyaret (etmek) 15d

waiter garson 11d
waiting room bekleme salonu 5a
Wales/Welsh Galler/Galli 2c
walk (to) yürü(mek) 16c
wallet cüzdan 9a, 20b
warm sıcak 17b
watch saat 8a
water su 10b, 14☐, 17b
water skiing su kayağı 16c
we biz Int.4
weather hava 17a,b,c
weather forecast hava tahmini 17a

English–Turkish Vocabulary

Wednesday Çarşamba 8c
welcome hoşgeldiniz 1b; buyrun 1c, 9c
well iyi 1b, 2a
well-done (cooked) iyi pişmiş 12b
west batı 4d
what ne Int.15, etc.
when ne zaman Int.15, 8b
where nerede Int.15, 4c, 4d, etc.
which hangi Int.15
white beyaz 19c
who(se) kim(in) Int.15
why niçin, neden Int.15
wife eş, karı(-m/-sı) 1f
wind rüzgar 17c

wine şarap 10b, 14b
wine list içki listesi 11b
with -ile Int.18, 1□, 6b, 14c
without -siz Int.18, 1□, 14c
woman kadın 1d
wood koru(luk) 16b

year yıl 8c
yellow sarı 19c
yes evet 1a, 2a
yesterday dün 8b
you siz (sen) Int.14, 1f
your(s) sizin(ki) Int.5, 1f
youth hostel gençlik yurdu 6a

First published 1989
Copyright © 1989 Necdet Teymur and Langenscheidt KG.
Adapted from the original format first published by
Langenscheidt 1983.

British Library Cataloguing in Publication Data

Teymur, Necdet
   Quick & easy Turkish—(Teach yourself books)
   1. Spoken Turkish language. Phrase books
   I. Title
   494′.3583421

ISBN 0340 50188 X

Phototypeset by Cotswold Typesetting Ltd, Gloucester
Printed and bound in Great Britain for
Hodder and Stoughton Educational,
a division of Hodder and Stoughton Ltd,
Mill Road, Dunton Green, Sevenoaks, Kent,
by Richard Clay Ltd, Bungay, Suffolk